The 3 Secret Pillars of Wealth

How to Crack Your Wealth Code Using the Tools of Self-made Billionaires

James Burns, Esq.

White Diamond Press

The 3 Secret Pillars of Wealth
Copyright © 2008 James Burns, Esq.
Published by White Diamond Press

All rights reserved. No part of this book may be reproduced (except for inclusion in reviews), disseminated or utilized in any form or by any means, electronic or mechanical, including photocopying, recording, or in any information storage and retrieval system, or the Internet/World Wide Web without written permission from the author or publisher.

This publication is designed to provide accurate and authoritative information in regard to the subject matter covered. It is sold with the understanding that neither the author nor the publisher is engaged in rendering financial, accounting, legal, or other professional services by publishing this book. If financial advice or other expert assistance is needed, the service of a competent professional should be sought. The author and publisher specifically disclaim any liability, loss or risk resulting from the use or application of the information contained in this book.

For more information, please contact:
jambur64@cox.net

Book design by:
Arbor Books, Inc.
www.arborbooks.com

Printed in the United States of America

The 3 Secret Pillars of Wealth
James Burns, Esq.

1. Title 2. Author 3. Personal Finance & Investing

Library of Congress Control Number: 2007941554

ISBN 10: 0-9801620-0-9
ISBN 13: 978-0-9801620-0-4

CONTENTS

Preface
Are You Really Prepared for Retirement?.....................v

Chapter One
Danger Ahead: Why Tradition Is No Longer Enough...................1

Chapter Two
Change Your Thinking, Change Your Life 5

Chapter Three
What Is an Investment? 9

Chapter Four
The Pie Chart: Beware of Asset Allocation 16

Chapter Five
The Fortuna Investment Triangle^{TM} 20

Chapter Six
What Are Your Real Market Returns? 23

Chapter Seven
Wealth Pillar One: Leverage 34

Chapter Eight
Wealth Pillar Two: Arbitrage....................42

Chapter Nine
Wealth Pillar Three: Cash Flow 51

Chapter Ten
Real Estate 59

Chapter Eleven
Life Insurance: The Misunderstood Asset 78

Chapter Twelve
The Five Steps Inside the Pillars of Wealth 93

Chapter Thirteen
Retirement Planning...102

Chapter Fourteen
Self-directed Pension Plans 120

Chapter Fifteen
Running Your Family Finances Like a Business........128

Chapter Sixteen
How Mortgage Management Can Create Wealth 137

Chapter Seventeen
Creating Your Financial Blueprint...............................166

Chapter Eighteen
Putting It All Together 166

Chapter Nineteen
How to Get the Ball Rolling..176

Appendix 183

PREFACE

Are You Really Prepared for Retirement?

> You cannot teach a man anything. You can only
> help him discover it within himself.
> —Galileo

Hope is not an investment strategy.

If you're like most people, you hope for a comfortable retirement doing what you like to do, free from financial worry. But have you asked yourself the tough questions that need answering before you can begin attaining your retirement goals? Do you even know, in specific detail, what your goals are? Do you want to live in the lap of luxury or merely continue living the lifestyle you currently enjoy? And do you know what it's going to take to be able to do those things?

Most people have never really taken a hard look at where they are financially and what it would take to reach their goals. That's because financial decisions are emotional and difficult, and change often involves risk. But change is what's needed if you want to start thinking and acting like someone in control of his or her finances. Investors think differently than non-investors and I need you start thinking like an investor if we're going to get your money to start working for you.

Before we get started, though, I want you to understand a few things about my approach to wealth building. While I believe that you can amass great wealth by sticking to these pillars of wealth, I don't want you thinking that this is a get-rich-quick book or that I expect you to immediately understand everything about wealth building just because you've read my book. This is going to take work and patience and planning, and maybe even help from a financial professional.

I believe in planning for the entire length of your lifetime, and that your plan will need updating and adjustment to survive as long as you do. Financially successful people understand that amassing wealth isn't about gimmicks or following the crowd. In order to create wealth you have to take a serious look at what's best for you and your family. There is no one-size-fits-all financial plan.

I'm going to ask you to think like a corporation and honestly look at your personal cash flow. Would you buy your family business as it is today, based on your personal balance sheet? Are you running the family finances to the best of your abilities, and are you using the Three Secret Pillars of Wealth? Recently, three of the richest men in the world were asked by *Forbes* magazine what the best investment advice that they'd ever heard was. Together, these three men identified the three pillars of wealth, and I want you to learn how to use them to the same great effect as these billionaires.

Similar to the many corporations that are now drafting vision statements, you need to have a clear vision of where you want to be, with goals that match that vision, before you can start implementing the three pillars.

Having a vision will be important to you as you plot your financial course. I think that its importance was best summed up by Helen Keller, who said, "It is a terrible thing to see and have no vision." That statement is powerful—it establishes the importance of using your vision of your future as a compass in order to reach your destination.

In addition to asking you to think about your vision, I'm also going to ask you to think in realistic terms about what you want to accomplish. When you set a financial goal it should be something you can achieve. Many people confuse having a goal with having an ideal. They have pictures in their minds of what the perfect world would be for them if they were multimillionaires. These ideals seem to change with time, place and circumstances. So, if you want to manifest a retirement with, say, $3 million, you're going to have to get clear about what it takes to get there, and support that goal with intention and work—not just hope.

I'm not saying that you shouldn't dream big or have lofty goals. I'm just saying that you need to be deliberate in the actions you take—and then, you can have what you want.

At first blush, running your home like a business may sound too intense, and taking a hard look at your finances may be too frightening. But no one is going to care more about your financial future than you are. The guy managing your company's 401(k) isn't going to sit down and plan your future for you. Following in the footsteps of a giant corporation and investing blindly in the stock market isn't going to make you rich, either. You need to invest in a way that's catered to your situation.

And you don't have to move blindly forward, either. You can adopt successful, proven strategies that have worked for billionaires and adapt them to your own businesses and personal finances. Just remember that running your business is not the same as running your family's ledger. When I tried running my family as I did my business, it became evident that I couldn't become the accountability officer in both places; I couldn't come down on my wife for overspending or otherwise mismanaging our cash flow, as I could with my employees. However, I found that I could absorb what was useful about accountability and use some of its guidelines to help my family stay on course with our financial vision.

Besides that, my wife has tempered my view on how much I can run my family like a corporation and still sleep with her, and not on the couch. I think we've found a happy medium that we are comfortable with; hopefully, you too will end up exploring your own limits.

You Have to Make Decisions

Investment decisions are hard and emotional because like any other decisions, they deal with change that could have consequences. The stakes are high in investing, and many people are fearful that a wrong step may place them so far in the red as to force bankruptcy. I hope to alleviate some of your worries through education, and with the recommendation that you make tiny steps toward your financial goals. I also want you to seriously consider seeking assistance from high-quality planners and investment coaches. As you achieve certain goals, you'll build your self-esteem and confidence, which increase your ability to make bigger and bolder decisions that lead to bigger and better results.

I wish I could tell you that you could achieve the kind of financial security you seek just by getting motivated and pumping yourself up, but the truth is that most people, especially successful investors, are highly motivated by some things and less motivated by others. Dan Sullivan of the Strategic Coach™ program suggests that rather than trying to get more motivated in general, it makes more sense to pay attention to what motivates you and then try to do more of it.

For example, if getting wealthy and living the lifestyle of your dreams motivates you, then go for it. If providing for your family and changing its economic tree for future generations motivates you, then let that drive you. On the other hand, if you are compelled by having an early and long retirement, and doing what you want to do while you're still vibrant and healthy, then make that your motivation.

Remember, this book is a tool—one of many you will need to use to plan successfully for yourself and your family. But, it also provides a fresh approach to investing that many people aren't yet aware exists. I believe in the use of tax-advantaged investment tools and a realistic approach to calculating your true earnings, and I'll show you which investment vehicles beat the traditional mutual fund when it comes to real return to the investor. Hopefully, along the way, you'll experience a real shift in thinking that will help you become a savvy investor for yourself and your family.

CHAPTER ONE

Danger Ahead: Why Tradition Is No Longer Enough

You're thirty-five years old and you earn $60,000 per year. If you want to retire in thirty years with the same lifestyle you're accustomed to now, you will need a $3,000,000 nest egg. Many people believe that this dollar figure is intimidating—a seemingly impossible mountain to scale. Others know that the three-million mark holds no other alternative. If you want to preserve your way of life, your American dream, you must focus; you must be responsible and you must be unrelenting in controlling your retirement's outcome.

A hundred years ago, only one in four Americans lived past the age of sixty-five. Today, three in four people surpass it. We expect to live longer now, and with the tremendous advances being made in medical science, life expectancies seem to be ever-increasing. Because of this, emerging generations are going to need more effective financial strategies—and because costs are rising while the value of the dollar is shrinking worldwide.

The last two generations in America—the immigrants and the baby boomers—had a different way of looking at life. They were taught four principals that were supposed to create success and happiness if followed correctly:

1. Get a college education
2. Get a job

3. Get married and start a family
4. Buy a house and pay it off as soon as you can, so you can be secure in your retirement

But the evidence is now clear that this formula no longer works in creating the kind of wealth the current generation of workers will need in retirement. The US Department of Health and Human Services says that thirty-six percent of sixty-five-year-olds are still working; fifty-four percent are dependent, requiring their family's or the government's assistance; five percent are deceased; and four percent are financially dependent with at least $3,000 per month to live on. One percent are wealthy.

With just a quick examination of the numbers, we can learn something from what that one percent is doing. Only ten percent of them are doctors and lawyers; another ten percent are CEOs and presidents. Five percent are top sales performers and one percent are lottery winners or people with nice inheritances. So, what do the other seventy-four percent of the successful one percent do for a living? They are business owners and real estate investors.

Success certainly leaves clues, but they are no longer found in the four-pronged advice of the traditional model. This is exemplified in the fact that ninety-nine percent of those who retire are not succeeding when it comes to their finances.

Wealth can translate into freedom and my hope is that through a better understanding of your options in our current economy, you'll be able to give yourselves more options in retirement. Our financial world is constantly changing and the old wisdom, valid in its time, is not enough in today's economy.

If the old path of education, job, marriage and home purchasing is the one you're on, and you believe that this formula is a sufficient economic strategy to acquire your $3,000,000 nest egg, I can assure you that as you read on, the facts will convince you otherwise. If you are open to examining the pitfalls of this traditional road to wealth and are willing to come to your own conclusion about its obsolescence, you will begin to be both a prudent investor and a retirement survivor. With disciplined practice, you can get into the one-percent club before retirement, or just in time for retirement.

The New Face of the Economy

People today switch jobs four times or more during their working years, to pursue higher salaries and better working conditions. Many people relocate five times or more in a career, perhaps even entirely across the country. Many are strapped with student loans or children to support, or saddled with high costs of living. Many live paycheck to paycheck. Some have two or more jobs to make ends meet, and have large personal debt. And the cost of a college education continues to escalate, putting more and more pressure on the household.

As a result of these various factors, many of us have trouble putting money away for retirement. Add to that the fact that job security is tenuous as technology changes the marketplace by the minute, and pressure builds from every angle. Let's face it: It's getting harder to keep up with the students who are vaulting from college armed with new and valuable information about computers and other technology.

And then, of course, there is the generally accepted notion that Social Security will be a dried-up dinosaur by the time we will be relying on it. The government is not planning for you; you have to plan for yourself. You, as an individual, need to manage your personal finances in a more creative, more aggressive manner or be faced with a future that is full of unknowns.

Many of you are either letting your available dollars sit around and gather dust or using your home equity like an ATM when you should be harvesting those equity dollars and putting them to work for your future. You are not fully optimized financially unless you're putting those lazy dollars to work.

In this book, I will teach you how to identify opportunities for better growth. But to do so, you and I have to accomplish a few things. First, we have to change the way you've been taught to think about making money. Second, we need to make sure that you know the difference between investing and speculating. Third, we need to make sure that you can understand why certain "investment" tools, like mutual funds, are just high finance's version of a street-side shell game.

Last, you need to understand why institutional models that are designed to protect the assets of large corporate entities do not make sense for individual investors. From there, I'll show you how to build a solid theory for your investment portfolio. This is based upon a theory of a close friend of mine—she calls it the Fortuna Triangle model of cash-flow dynamics.

When you have a good grasp of that, I will take you through the Three Secret Pillars of Wealth. These principals are not secret scrolls hidden in some ancient tomb. The Three Secret Pillars of Wealth are sound principals. They are the tools of self-made billionaires, who have used them to create wealth. Once you understand how the pillars connect and interact, you will be on your way to creating vast amounts of wealth for you and your children. I am pleased to be able to reveal these hidden pillars, to help you achieve the life and retirement you wish for.

What We Learned

1. We have to change the way you've been taught to think about making money.

2. We need to make sure that you know the difference between investing and speculating.

3. We need to make sure that you can understand why some common investment vehicles are not what they appear to be.

4. Seventy-four percent of the one percent who become wealthy in retirement are business owners and real estate investors.

5. Success leaves clues.

CHAPTER TWO

Change Your Thinking, Change Your Life

Money, wampum, the almighty dollar, greenbacks, dinero, cold hard cash. When we use words like these, we all get instant images in our heads, but the investor thinks differently when discussing money.

Many Americans—the non-investors—see money as a means to get new possessions—such as grand vacations, fancy cars and designer clothes. They don't imagine that money is so much more than that. They do not see the opportunities that money can create, or the capabilities that it has. By the time we're done here, you will not only see what money can do; you'll understand it, and you will be an investor.

The Investor Mindset

Investors see money as a tool—they invest a lot today and buy a lot more tomorrow. Non-investors buy today and pay a lot more tomorrow. In essence, our social stratification or classes have very different spending patterns. If you don't change your pattern, it is more difficult to change your class. Whether or not you do this is up to you.

To people who are financially broke, investing is not a priority and so they don't keep anything to invest. It's something many people don't budget into their lives. They budget for clothes, going out, vacations, televisions and nice cars that depreciate the minute they roll off the lot. Non-investors budget around those things and don't focus on how to grow their money.

Investors, on the other hand, budget around investments, believing that their money should work for them. This is different from non-investors, who believe that they should work for their money.

Non-investors wish that they had better jobs that paid more money, so that they could be rich and buy more things. It's circular logic, and by having that attitude, many people are hurting their long-term chances for success.

During my years as a wealth advisor and estate-planning attorney, I've helped all kinds of people, from investors to average people who simply want to avoid probate taxes upon their death. In all of my experience, one thing that has rung true time and time again is that there is a clear difference in the manner of thinking between the poor middle class and the wealthy, and that thinking is a state of mind and a matter of practice.

Often, poor and middle-class people don't look beyond the opportunities afforded through their employers. They adopt a mindset that is limiting and ill informed. They have 401(k) plans that their employers don't contribute to, as well as certificates of deposit and mutual funds, and they believe that these are good ways to go about securing their futures.

Pure investors are very different in their thinking and practice. They use their money to make more money. They take some risks to do it, but they understand that without risk, there can be no reward.

I would encourage people who are not satisfied with their financial positions in life, and who do not want to work until they are in their eighties, to make some drastic mental shifts. You *can* create a roadmap for this journey we call life. Like any other voyager, without a map, you will simply float aimlessly.

The right map has to be charted properly and must take advantage of proven wealth-building techniques, such as the Three Secret Pillars of Wealth. They are secret only in that most people are unaware of their power and how available they are. The real key to being a solid investor is maximizing the opportunities to use them and reclaiming their benefits as much as possible.

Mental Pitfalls

Number one—and this is going to be a hard pattern to change overnight, but you need to try—has to do with credit. There are currently more than 641 million high-interest credit cards in circulation in the United States, and the number is growing every year. These are not a prudent means of making your money work for you. Paying high interest to someone simply to avoid going to the ATM is crazy—it really is. You need to get your credit card balances to zero unless the charges are tax-deductible, such as materials for your business. Credit card companies have made careless customers of the majority of Americans and if you are one of these people, you need to change that.

The history of credit cards is interesting, and it helps explain why they were created, and why some people have total reliance on them. In 1946, John Biggins of the Flatbush National Bank of Brooklyn created the first bank-issued credit card, called the "Charge-It" program, to facilitate transactions between bank customers and local merchants. Around 1950, Diners Club issued their credit card in the United States. In 1958, American Express issued their first credit card and Bank of America issued the BankAmericard (now Visa).

Originally, the cards were to be used by businesses that had deductible expenses. The cards were first promoted to traveling salesmen for use on the road, and the idea quickly caught on.

It is important to note that in the '60s, '70s and early '80s, there were no ATMs. If you did not extricate your cash from the bank by Saturday morning, you had no purchasing power until Monday morning—unless, of course, you used your credit card. This quickly became the method of payment in restaurants and stores, as the enticement to pay later for what you could put in your hands today was overwhelming.

It became commonplace to find several couples out to dinner, with one person, who may have had a bit too much to drink, whisking a credit card out of his pocket and declaring, "Dinner is on me." That was all well and good in the friendly confines of social behavior but when the bill came at the end of the month, and only a partial payment was made for the over-budgeted expense, large amounts of interest were tacked on, leaving the potential investor not only cash poor but perhaps swimming in debt.

I know I'm not going to convince most of you to go cold turkey overnight without the drastic plastic, but each time you use it, think about the best use of the credit card, which is anything that makes you more money—such as business assets or investments in infrastructure that will eventually pay for themselves. Also, reservations and emergencies are acceptable uses for a credit card. Leave the rest for something you have in your pocket: cold hard cash.

In order to get wealthy, you need to take control and eliminate the debt that is holding you back. Sometimes, this can be as easy as coming to terms with it and seeing it in a manageable way in front of you. There is also a fantastic product out there that helps with debts and paying off your mortgage in half the time, but we'll talk more about that in Chapter Fifteen.

What We Learned

1. Investors see money as a tool to invest; non-investors buy today and pay a lot more tomorrow.

2. Pure investors are very different from the average person in their thinking and practice. They use their money to make more money. They take some risks to do it, but they understand that without risk, there can be no reward.

3. The best use of a credit card is anything that makes you more money, such as deductible business expenses. It is also acceptable to use credit when making reservations, or in the case of emergencies.

4. Eliminate debts by using software or Websites like http://www.debtmd.com. If your situation is really bad, turn to debt counseling—just do something.

CHAPTER THREE

What Is an Investment?

What does the word "investment" mean to you? Benjamin Graham, once called the "dean of Wall Street" and a mentor to celebrated investor Warren Buffet, believed that a true investment has two components:

1. Safety of principal
2. Adequate return

Anything not meeting both components is considered pure speculation, which is ninety-five percent of what Wall Street offers. When I look at prospective client portfolios loaded down with stocks and mutual funds that are down ten percent, twenty percent or more, I ask the clients if they are comfortable with that. When they say, "Yes, you know, the market goes up and down," I have to shake my head. People have become complacent with losses. But that is not the way to build wealth.

Speculative investments often come from word of mouth. For example, you get a "tip" from a friend working for a company. Or, one of the members of your golf foursome has "inside information." Maybe you overhear something at a local restaurant. All of these are speculative and put your money at risk. You might as well fly to Las Vegas, close your eyes and bet on black or red—that way, you'll have more fun while losing your money.

Alongside Mr. Graham's two-pronged test, I submit that there is a third component that identifies the characteristics of proper investment:

the liquidity of the asset. Liquidity is the ability to turn your asset into cash in a fast manner. For example, if a real estate broker tells you that your house is worth $300,000 and six months later, you haven't gotten an offer on it, you do not have a liquid asset. On the other hand, if you've extracted equity from that property and placed it in a side fund, you've transformed an illiquid asset into a very liquid one.

Why is this important? If you want your money to be in play—that is, earning more money—you must be able to create cash instantly, or you will miss opportunities that can be exploited through the Three Secret Pillars of Wealth.

The following is a partial list of the most common assets in which people invest:

Commodities: These are tangible goods that can be sold or traded. Corn, wheat and soybeans are commodities, as are gold, silver and other precious metals.

Business ventures: The guy down the street is starting a new computer software company in his garage and he needs some money to fuel the business.

Limited partnerships: These are a means of investing in a business without being responsible for any of the liabilities that may arise.

Investment real estate: This is sometimes a corporation that pools its investors' money to purchase and manage income properties—or, you can acquire your own portfolio of rental properties.

Deeds of trust: This is a legal instrument that is transferred to you when you loan someone money to secure a property. It is similar to a mortgage.

Speculative common stocks: These are the stocks traded daily on the NYSE, NASDAQ, S&P and Dow Jones.

Lower-quality bonds: A bond is basically a note guaranteeing repayment by a certain date of the principal and, usually, interest. The advantage of a bond is that it has priority over stockholders when money is distributed, should there be financial difficulties. Lower-quality bonds are high-risk, high-return bonds. You may know them as "junk bonds" from the Michael Milken days.

Blue-chip stocks: These are the big boys—high-priced stocks that have the public's faith because of long-term performances. Johnson & Johnson is a fine example. Due to products and structure, there is little risk that the company will fold overnight.

High-grade bonds: This is a bond with limited risk. There are two companies that rate bonds: Standard & Poor's and Moody's. To be high-grade, a bond must be rated 3AAA or 2AA.

Mutual funds: A single company gets large groups of people together to put money into their fund. They then invest that money in stocks with the hope that the size of their position can create greater returns. There are a lot of hidden costs that can kill your return in these situations; they are described later on in this book.

CDs: Certificates of deposit are low-risk, low-return engines. You can buy ninety-day CDs from your bank. If you withdraw money prematurely, you are penalized.

Investment-grade insurance: With this, you put X amount of dollars per month into a policy that is indexed to the S&P. For over half a century, the S&P has yielded eight percent. However, when this index is used inside the insurance wrapper, that same eight percent is accumulated tax-free—a very big significance.

Money market funds: An open-ended fund that only invests in money markets for very short periods of time. No risk *per se*, but low returns. This is often where investors stash non-invested cash as a money market fund is very liquid and can be summoned quickly.

US Treasury bills—also referred to as "T-bills": These are notes that last less than one year and are auctioned by the US government to raise funds. They are not interest-producing, but here's the catch: They are sold below value, which is called PAR, and then when they are purchased back, they are purchased *at* PAR.

Annuities: Contracts sold by insurance companies that pay out after a certain time and are not taxed until dividends are paid out. These can meet the Graham two-pronged test because they preserve principal (as long as it's not variable) and provide adequate return with tax deferral.

Home equity: This is simple—it's the amount owed upon your house versus the market value of the house. Let's say you owe $50,000 on your home and it's valued at $350,000. You have the potential to borrow $300,000 at the bank's low interest rate and turn that around into another one of the investments listed above, to grab a higher yield.

Tax lien certificates: If someone fails to pay property taxes, the government can put a lien on their property and then auction the debt in order to recoup their money. The property owner then has a redemption period to pay the back taxes—plus interest—to the new owner of the debt, which could be you, if you purchase it at auction. If they don't pay, they could face foreclosure.

The point of the three-pronged standard for a great investment—liquidity, safety of principal, and adequate return—is to apply it to investment opportunities as a litmus test. If you remember from above, we defined liquidity as the ability to turn your asset into cash in a fast manner. If we add the test of liquidity to the list of popular investments that we defined above, the group shrinks to the following:

1. Commodities
2. Speculative common stocks
3. Lower-quality bonds
4. Blue-chip stocks
5. High-grade bonds
6. Mutual funds
7. CDs
8. Investment-grade insurance
9. Tax lien certificates
10. US Treasury bills
11. Annuities

So, you see, we lost five of the most popular asset investments on liquidity alone. If we then apply the safety of principal prong to the group, we are left with the following:

1. Blue-chip stocks
2. High-grade bonds
3. Mutual funds
4. CDs
5. Investment-grade insurance
6. Tax lien certificates
7. US Treasury bills
8. Annuities

Now we are down to only eight assets that fit our three prongs, after only testing for safety and liquidity. If we apply the other prong, adequate return, we get into something that is subjective to every individual. It is my opinion that the bonds, the stocks and even the mutual funds will do less than many of the insurances and annuities, and certainly less than tax lien certificates.

As you can see, the purpose of this filter is to quickly assess assets according to time-honored principals that seem to have evaporated on Wall Street, and to let you judge what you believe to be a truly worthwhile investment of your hard-earned money.

As listed above, there are all manner of investments. Sadly, many Americans are never educated by our wonderful school systems on how these investments work and what benefit can be gained from them. The general rule is that you can expect bonds to give you a four- to five-percent return. Precious metals can give you a three- to four-percent return. Stocks can give you a nine- to ten-percent return.

Now, so we don't jump too far ahead, a return is the amount of money you get above and beyond the amount of money you invested. For example, if you invested $10,000 in bonds with a five-percent rate of return, it would take you ninety-four years to reach $1 million. If you put your money in an index fund, which basically tracks the stock market, and you were getting a ten-percent return, it would take you forty-eight years.

It's easy to get greedy when looking at potential returns. You have to be careful when viewing them, and use good judgment. Some folks—many of them late-night infomercial charlatans—will show you how to get extraordinary yields with futures (future contracts to buy commodities or other financial instruments at a certain price) and options, which involves betting on whether a certain stock will go up (a call) or down (a put).

As in life, use your common sense and remember that if something sounds too good to be true, it's probably a scam. If people were getting twenty-five percent returns on their money all the time, no one would be working. There are some good systems that will give you a two- or three-percent edge. Therefore, instead of a ten-percent return, you'll get twelve or thirteen percent, which is pretty good. However, this only brings the time down to thirty or thirty-five years to turn $10,000 into $1 million, and remember, our goal is to have $3 million worth of liquid assets by that thirty-year marker.

Growth stocks can give you over a seventeen-percent return, but they won't do it consistently, and they're very risky. Even if you could get that much consistently, it would still take you twenty-nine years to turn $10,000 into a million, and that just doesn't meet the goal.

If you can invest more than $10,000, it obviously reduces your wealth-time horizon. If, let's say, you had $50,000 to invest, and you got a five-percent return on your investment (ROI), it would take you sixty-one years instead of ninety-four to grab that $1 million. If you were able to get a seventeen-percent ROI, it would still take you nineteen years.

So, the point is obvious: We need a method to gain higher returns over a shorter period of time, so that we can reinvest that returned or harvested money in a continuous loop, without any lazy money lying around—that is, money that is not being optimally used. Then, thirty years later, we will have our needed nest egg.

And how do we do this? We do it one step at a time in a careful manner, which is why the next chapter is about investment models to stay away from.

What We Learned

1. A true investment has two components:
    a. Safety of principal
    b. Adequate return

2. Look for liquidity when you can find it in addition to those two components.

3. We need a method to gain higher returns over a shorter period of time so that we can reinvest that returned or harvested money in a continuous loop.

CHAPTER FOUR

The Pie Chart: Beware of Asset Allocation

Let us always remember that you are an individual investor, not a multinational corporation. You are not a large finance company on Wall Street. You do not care how the person standing next to you is doing in the market. You care about yourself and your bottom line, and you should invest that way.

But this is difficult at the start of the twenty-first century because there are many perceived truths about investing that do not apply to the individual investor, although the average money-hungry broker wants you to believe that they do. Large organizations that are able to sustain themselves with minimal growth have developed a means of investing for the long haul, reducing their risk and return. Your life is not that long. You need to create that $3,000,000 nest egg you've targeted in a short period of time—just thirty to forty years. You don't have time to wait the hundred years for your investments to pay off, like a large corporate entity does.

With a short history lesson, you can see why the popular investment strategies of the '90s and the new millennium are not tailored toward the needs of your future. In 1952, a man name Harry Markowitz wrote a graduate thesis paper called "Portfolio Selection." This well-written piece ended up in a publication named the *Journal of Finance*, a widely read publication in the field. As new ideas sometimes do, it took quite a while for people to take his ideas to heart, but when the market experienced a large hiccup during the sessions of 1973 and 1974, and people were angered by their widespread losses, Markowitz's ideas surfaced again.

The premise of his thesis was that if you were involved in only one or two stocks and one happened to go under, you were in serious trouble. He then theorized that if you owned a variety of stocks spread over various industries and one happened to plummet, it was more than likely that another stock, in another industry in your portfolio, would pick up the slack and cover your back.

Simply put, the more stocks you owned, the less risk exposure you would have when it came to financial disaster. If one stock went bad, it would only be a small percentage of what you owned and thus, you wouldn't lose your total capital; if another area you were invested in happened to perform well you would, in a bad situation, break even or better. This became known as diversification.

Markowitz continued to work on this theory and was awarded the Nobel Prize in 1990 for his continued exploration of portfolio theories. The follow-up to his work that kept this idea of diverse asset allocation alive and flourishing was the Brinson, Hood and Beebower study of 1986. It appeared in the *Financial Analysts Journal*, July/August 1986, and was revamped in 1991.

In this ten-year study, the three gentlemen followed ninety-one pension plans and argued that for that decade-long period, investors were better off with an asset mix of stocks, bonds and cash. Although the study took many things for granted, the theory became the word on the street, with large companies investing here, there and everywhere to balance their risk exposure over the long haul.

This variegated approach to ownership became known as the "pie chart," because investors were shown their widely diverse portfolios on colored pie charts that seemed to explain why they were no longer at risk of a down market. As a keen adviser, you can trace this love of the pie chart to the time's increasing popularity of the personal computer, which allowed the average investor to create colored charts at will, making the new idea of pie charts that much more flashy and impressive—even if they were truly suspect to you and me.

For individual investors, the fundamental problem with BHB's analysis is that it focuses on explaining portfolio volatility rather than portfolio returns. If you have no risk and no return, what's the point? We're trying to generate money, not sit tight and let inflation run us over.

Another flaw with this model is that it ignores real property. For many of us, our homes or other investment properties make up ninety percent of our portfolios; for most of us, our residences are the main cornerstones of our portfolios. The problem is, the BHB study was designed for institutions with 100-percent-investible assets—not for you and me, individual investors who have lifestyle needs and expenses.

In short, the asset allocation model—the pie chart with so many stocks and bonds and perhaps three percent cash—is an out-and-out failure for the individual investor. You have to adjust your thinking to understand what it does and what it does not do. You must realize that if you have great investments, there is no reason to weigh them down with bad ones.

Why You Won't See Real Estate in the Average Pie Chart

You'll rarely see real estate in a pie chart created by a financial advisor, even though your home equity may be worth far more than anything else in your portfolio. Investment advisors do not offer you the idea of buying investment properties that appreciate, allowing you to harvest dollars out of them by way of refinancing and rents and then re-harvest by doing the same cycle over and over, increasing your wealth along with tax deductions.

Why do they not recommend this? Because if they did, no one would be buying their multifaceted investment schemes, like mutual funds, that get their managers fat in the pocketbook but barely get you over the inflation return line.

I realize that seems like a bold statement, but if you can understand why the pie chart model may not be smart for you, you will be able to understand why the theory of the Fortuna Triangle, developed by my close friend, Karen Brenner, is a much simpler manner of investing that targets the individual investor—YOU—instead of the large, corporate entity.

A 2005 Harvard University study, *Housing Wealth and Retirement Savings: Enhancing Financial Security for Older Americans*, determined that residential real estate has grown to become the largest single-asset class held by households with heads aged sixty-five or older. More than eighty percent of senior citizens owned a home, and residential real estate accounted for thirty percent of the group's aggregate asset holdings, according to the study.

By contrast, only twenty-one percent of all households with heads sixty-five and older owned stocks. The study also found that real estate equity was more widely distributed across all income levels than were stock market investments. If this is the case, why are financial planners still showing people the pie chart and not allowing real estate and other assets to be a part of their clients' retirements? The answer is: Because it is not a part of their compensation grid.

The equity in a home has to be seen as the only asset in home ownership. Robert Kiyosaki, author of *Rich Dad Poor Dad*,[1] believes that a home is a liability and I think it is, too, unless you're using it as an asset—and that means deploying unused equity.

Let's examine this for a moment. What asset has a zero rate of return, is illiquid, forces you to qualify based on income and pays no interest, and yet most everyone has it? The answer is: your home. A home is an asset that violates every rule I'm trying to teach you, unless you use the equity in it for solid investments that do follow the rules. And yet, people sit on their homes, getting nothing in return; often, as in many disaster situations, they even leave it all on the table, to be taken by one tragic event. The victims of Hurricane Katrina, the Laguna Beach landslide and the earthquakes in Hawaii all wish they'd had their equity outside of the home, working for them in an independent fund, rather than leaving themselves vulnerable to a natural disaster.

What We Learned

The fundamental problem with pie chart allocation is that it focuses on explaining portfolio volatility rather than portfolio returns.

1. Why don't investment advisors offer you the idea of buying investment properties? Because it is not a part of their compensation grid.

---

[1] Robert Kiyosaki, "Rich Dad Poor Dad" (New York: Warner Books, 2000), 15

CHAPTER FIVE

The Fortuna Investment Triangle™

Institutions and individuals both run their financial lives on cash flow—revenue, income, gross receipts, dividends and interest versus cost and expenses. Institutions have long-term (hopefully consistent) cash flow sources, usually from business or investors. Individuals typically have long-term cash flow requirements (you need money through the end of your life) and short-term cash flow sources (usually, your working life).

Consequently, the investing and portfolio-building strategy for an individual, a family trust, or an individual retirement plan needs to take into account a cash flow component that is different than an institution's. Investing strategies for institutions rely on the fact that they have long-term cash flow and that, as a long-lived entity, they can take advantage of stock market cycles over forty-plus years. An individual typically cannot take advantage of these long-term strategies. Essentially, life is too short.

Triangle practitioners believe that individual investors should not be thinking in terms of institutional strategies. Instead, individuals should build portfolios with strategies that meld with their own financial practices, with the way they live and plan to

Fortuna Investment Triangle™ "FIT"

live. First and foremost, they must not lose principal; second, they must invest for cash flow to meet expenses; and third, they must invest for growth with specified funds and excess cash flow.

A simple way to picture this strategy is by using the Fortuna Investment Triangle™ ("FIT"), which is divided into three general tiers, each supported by the one below. The base is comprised of cash flow investments; the proportion of this tier to the rest of the triangle is generally around sixty percent, but is calculated from an individual's needs. The second tier represents low-risk growth investments and generally accounts for around thirty-five percent of the triangle. A third tier, the smallest at around five percent of the triangle, is reserved for speculative or high-risk growth investments.

FIT™ can also be used to evaluate the health of the allocations in a portfolio. Every investment fits somewhere in the triangle. When evaluating a portfolio—by this, I mean all holdings including real estate, loans, gems, coins and cash, not just stocks and bonds—often, the hard part is identifying the true risks. Once they are identified, however, the investment can be categorized and depicted on the triangle.

For many portfolios, the resulting picture is not healthy. The proportions are often off, with speculative investments covering most of the triangle and cash flow investments comprising a small, often miniscule layer at the bottom—which does not offer much support.

Below, you will see depictions of the triangle as used for planning investments and as an icon to readily identify the type of investment:

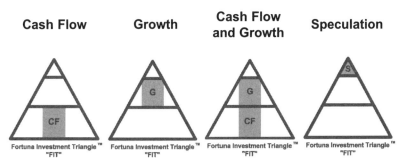

In tandem with the Fortuna Triangle, I've created the Burns Financial Planning Quadrant, which provides a device to examine all aspects of a client's financial being, so that nothing is missed. You'll see my quadrant in Chapter Seventeen.

What We Learned

1. The individual investor cannot invest as a large institution would.

2. Individual investors should focus mostly on cash flow.

CHAPTER SIX

What Are Your Real Market Returns?

In recent years, mutual funds have gained popularity as the push for "diversification" has led many to believe that a broad range of investments is the best way to secure consistent returns in an often-volatile market.

Most people assume that mutual funds require little effort and promise consistent returns. The reality can often be very different because of the fees charged by the fund managers and because of the quick and easy practice of placing clients into an equity fund without real thought.

Often, planners will place you into a fund without really considering your situation, thinking that the funds will provide a simple form of diversification that requires little thought. The planner you choose—or the one whom someone refers you to—will often check your pulse for risk and then make the selection for you. Worse yet, he or she may have you select the funds for your retirement account yourself. As you will read later in this chapter, you'll find out how well these funds work—or, more appropriately, don't work—for long-term planning like retirement.

A Brief History of Investment Funds
The idea of pooling money together for investment purposes seems to have started in Europe in the mid-1800s. The first pooled investment fund in America was founded in 1893, put together for the faculty and staff of Harvard. On March 21, 1924, the first official mutual fund was born. It was called the Massachusetts Investors

Trust and it came to life when three Boston securities executives pooled their money together, not knowing how popular and lucrative the funds would become for the financial companies that peddled them.

Recent Views on Mutual Funds

In recent commentary, insiders have adopted a more skeptical outlook on mutual funds. Richard Rutner, author of *The Trouble With Mutual Funds*, said in 2002 that "most investors in mutual funds have no idea what they are invested in, which is the way the industry wants it."[2] Others have said that mutual funds are flawed because the fund managers are rewarded for the amount of money they draw to the fund, not the amount of money they earn for the investors in the fund.[3]

SEC Chairman Arthur Levitt, Jr. warned of growing unfairness in the relationship between individual investors and mutual funds in January 2001. Mr. Levitt made the following comment:

There are a number of instances that, quite frankly, do not honor an investor's rights. Instances where…hidden costs hurt an investor's bottom line, where spin and hype mask the true performance of a mutual fund, and where accounting tricks and sleight of hand dresses up a fund's financial results.[4]

What most people don't know is that there are five separate bills that mutual funds charge.[5] The best way to determine if an investment will be effective for you or not is to dollarize the benefit or the burden. When you invest in the typical mutual fund, assuming it is outside of a qualified retirement plan, you face costs that erode your benefit. Chances are, you're not aware of them; they're not in your

---

[2] Richard Rutner, The Trouble With Mutual Funds (Seattle: Elton-Wolf Publishing, 2002), p 2-3.
[3] George Soros, from his speech "The Case for an Open Society," April 23, 1997. Soros is famously known for breaking the Bank of England on Black Wednesday in 1992. With an estimated current net worth of around $8.5 billion, he is ranked by Forbes as the twenty-seventh-richest person in America.
[4] Arthur Levitt, "Speech by SEC Chairman: The Future for America's Investors—Their Rights and Obligations," US Securities and Exchange Commission, http://www.sec.gov/news/speech/spch457.htm.
[5] Rutner, 57.

prospectus and your broker isn't going to sit down and tell you about them.

The five costs of mutual fund investing are:

1. Tax costs: excessive capital gains from active trading.

2. Transaction costs: the cost of the trades themselves.

3. Opportunity costs: dollars taken out of portfolios for a fund's safekeeping.

4. Sales charges: both seen and hidden.

5. Expense ratio, or "management fees": no end to increases in site. This is a calculation based on the operating costs of the fund divided by the average amount of assets under management.

How do fund expenses affect you? Well, with the expense ratio, which averages 1.6 percent per year, sales charges of 0.5 percent, turnover-generated portfolio transaction costs of 0.7 percent, and opportunity costs of 0.3 percent—when funds hold cash rather than remain fully invested in stocks—average mutual fund investors lose 3.1 percent of their investment returns every year just on fees. While this might not seem like much on the surface, costs and fees alone could consume thirty-one percent of a ten-percent market return.

Think about that. You could be losing almost a third of your return before it's even taxed, just for the cost of maintaining your investment. Add in the 1.5 percent capital gains tax bill that the average fund investor pays each year and that figure shoots up to forty-six percent of your return that is lost to fees and expenses—nearly half of a potential ten-percent return.[6] When you hear that, don't you feel like you're taking one or two steps back instead of going forward?

---

[6] Bogle Financial Markets Research Center, "The Wall Street Casino," Vanguard, http://www.vanguard.com/bogle_site/sp19990823.htm.

According to Richard Rutner, "The vast majority of mutual funds (ninety-four percent according to a recent five-year survey by Lipper Analytical Services) have underperformed the stock market as a whole."[7]

Part of the problem with uninformed investors is that they believe most of what they hear about mutual funds. There are several misconceptions about mutual funds that people have come to believe. It's important for you as an investor to understand some of these misconceptions so that you can see the big picture when investing your money.

One of the most common misconceptions people have about funds is that they are places to store money for the long-term. But, the record shows that many funds simply collapse, leaving investors in the lurch.

Another misconception about funds is that the managers of these funds are long-term thinkers, planning for years down the road, when you'll retire. The truth is that most funds experience huge turnover in their investments.

If the fund managers are short-term investors, then surely, the investors themselves are interested in staying put. But, like the managers, many investors in these funds are in and out, never staying long enough to experience any long-term gains. And because mutual funds have become so prevalent, many people think they've become cheaper. Again, that just doesn't stand up to scrutiny. Many funds now charge double what they did several decades ago.

And if the increasing management fees weren't enough, the fact is that most funds just aren't returning the kind of earnings that investors deserve. The simple truth is that the managers of these funds aren't any better at beating the market than you or I.

If you're convinced that you want to rely on stock market gains, remember to follow John Bogle's formula for calculating your returns: cumulative long-term returns earned by business = annual dividend yield + annual rate of earnings growth.[8]

---

[7] Rutner, 7
[8] John C. Bogle, The Little Book of Common Sense Investing (Hoboken: Wiley, 2007), 68.

In the long run, stock returns depend almost entirely on the reality of the investment returns earned by corporations. The perceptions of investors reflect speculative returns, but economics controls long-term equity returns; emotions, so dominant in the short-term, don't play a major role in the actual return on investment.

After subtracting the cost of managing the fund—management fees, brokerage commissions, sales loads, advertising costs and operating costs—return to the investors as a group falls short of the market return. In a market that returns ten percent as a gross return, what is the actual return to the investor after expenses? It turns out that it's not very good.

In equity funds, the expense ratio, which is the management fee and operating expenses combined, averages about 1.5 percent per year of fund assets. Add another half percent in sales charges, assuming that a five-percent initial sales charge is spread over a ten-year holding period. If the shares are held for five years, the cost will be twice that figure.[9]

Add to this the fact that the average fund turns its portfolio over at a rate of 100 percent per year and you're looking at another one percent in fees. How does this work? Well, say a $10 billion fund buys $10 billon of stocks each year and sells another $10 billion. At that rate, brokerage commissions, bid-ask spreads (the difference between the bid price and the sale price of a stock), and market impact costs add a major layer of additional cost.[10] In the end, the cost could be as high as 3 to 3.5 percent per year for expenses.

It's important to think of all this math as a blueprint by which you can gauge how successful your investment in a fund has really been. If your returns, after management fees and taxes, don't surpass the rate of inflation, then you might as well have stuck your money in a savings account.

There is also the problem of dollar-weighted returns, which is when money flows into a fund after a good performance, or out on a bad performance. Essentially, funds experience tides in the rate of

---

[9] Rutner, 37.
[10] Bogle, 37.

participation in them, based on how well they've done, and the rate at which this happens is a good way to measure a fund's rate of growth.

Another problem associated with equity funds is the adverse selection and faulty timing of stock picks for the fund, which often involves stocks that are overvalued. In other words, managers can screw up and pay too much for a stock, or simply pick a stock at the wrong time.

Do you think it's possible for the manager of a fund to buy an asset at the wrong time and overpay for it? The answer is yes. In the words of Bogle, "Adverse fund selection will likely continue to bedevil the typical fund shareholder's outcome."[11]

Because of all of these mistakes, it's important that you look at funds from the perspective of the actual individual investor return, which is the real amount of your earnings if you factor in inflation, taxes and expenses. Investing in mutual funds can be a defeating process and I would urge anyone whose primary retirement or investment strategy is packed with funds to find out how much, exactly, it is costing them. Planning for your retirement is generally long-term and as you've seen, many funds are not long-term propositions.

Your current financial planner may disagree with the preceding statements and that is fine, but just ask him to sit down with you and plot out all the costs of your fund, including taxes, inflation and fund expenses, to see where you land. You might be surprised by how much your funds are costing you, as opposed to what they're earning for you.

If you want more proof, consider a study performed by Bogle of 355 equity funds and their performances in the last thirty-five years, which is about the length of time a person would work prior to retirement. The results of Bogle's careful research revealed that the equity funds, all started in 1970, had a track record that looked like this:

---

[11] Bogle, 72.

- Almost two-thirds of those funds—that's 223 of them—are gone. They simply don't exist anymore.
- Sixty of the equity funds remain, but they underperform the S&P 500 by more than one percent per year.
- Forty-eight equity funds provided returns within one percent, plus or minus, of the S&P.
- Twenty-four of the equity funds—that's just one out of every fourteen—outpaced the market by more than one percent.
- Fifteen of those twenty-four outpaced the market by less than two percent per year, which is likely due to dumb luck as much as skill.
- The other nine, the solid, long-term winners, outpaced the market by two percent.
- However, six of the nine achieved their superiority years ago, when they were small.
- One fund peaked in 1982 and has lagged ever since.
- Two others peaked in 1983.
- The remaining three peaked in 1993, more than a decade ago, including Magellan, which has now struggled for twelve consecutive years.[12]

Only three funds out of the 355 that started in 1970—just eight-tenths of one percent—both survived and created a record of sustained value. If you're interested in finding out what those funds are, you can contact my office or pick up Mr. Bogle's book for yourself.

Even though those three made it, though, what does that mean for the next thirty-five years? Bogle stated that since the business and political environments change so rapidly, expectations based on past events are becoming less and less useful.[13] To assume that a fund that had prior success can continue that ride into the future is pure speculation.

---
[12] Bogle, 82.
[13] Bogle, 81–83.

Accordingly, when you consider the current market dividend rate, and that the average return from the market as a whole is just two percent since the amazing run-up we had in 1999, there should be little doubt that returns will be lower going forward because of the less robust market. The 2.5-percent cost on a seven-percent return would consume forty percent of it, and nearly sixty percent of a 4.5-percent real return on stocks.[14] I ask you again, is investing in equity funds the right thing to do with your hard-earned dollars if you need to make headway for retirement in the next decade or two?

Certificates of Deposit

The traditional "income investment" for tens of millions of Americans has been and remains CDs—certificates of deposit. However, after taxes, many people earn less than three percent per year on their CDs, which is less than the rate of inflation.

When a person invests in a CD, it can actually make them poorer each year because their earnings aren't outpacing the weakening of the dollar to inflation. To demonstrate why this is, we have to go back in time, learn a brief history lesson and gain an understanding of inflation.

Inflation is the rate at which the general level of prices for goods and services rises while purchasing power subsequently falls. As inflation rises, every dollar will buy a smaller percentage of a good. For example, if the inflation rate is two percent, then a pack of gum that costs one dollar today will cost $1.02 in a year. For further illustration, great inflation calculators can be found online at http://www.westegg.com/inflation and http://inflationdata.com/Inflation/Inflation_Rate/HistoricalInflation.aspx.

In 1971, President Nixon cancelled the Bretton Woods system, an agreement signed in Bretton Woods, New Hampshire, that had tied the value of major currencies to gold. At the same time as Nixon's decision, more money was being spent overseas by both the government and private investors. Because the dollar was becoming weaker, many countries started asking for gold in exchange for the dollars they held at the time.

---

[14] Bogle, 81–83.

On August 15, 1971, Nixon responded to those demands by imposing wage and price controls, and a ten percent import surcharge. Nixon also made a decision that is still affecting the economy today, as well as your own savings: He made it impossible for people to convert their paper money to gold, except on the open market.

The consequences of Nixon's actions have been far ranging. Former Federal Reserve chairman Alan Greenspan said he believed that in the absence of the gold standard, people's savings were being "confiscated" through inflation.

But the government isn't likely to change the system back. If they did, traditional savings in the form of bank notes could become worthless, should a large percentage of the population decide to switch to gold, or should merchants decide to stop accepting cash and checks.[15]

What this all means for you is that holding cash in a bank is actually detrimental to your overall financial picture because money that's just sitting still is losing value to inflation.[16]

As an example of how useless CDs and other cash holdings can be, just take a look at what happened in the 70s and 80s. From 1970–74, the rate of return on six-month certificates of deposit (CDs) rose from 7.64 percent to 10.02 percent, which thrilled investors. Then, the rates of return increased again in 1979, going from 11.42 percent to 15.79 percent by 1981. But what was the real rate of return that these happy investors received on their money? Turns out it wasn't as good as they thought.

In 1980, inflation rose to more than 13.5 percent while CDs paid out just 12.94 percent. CDs were losing value when it came to their real spending power.[17]

---

[15] Alan Greenspan, "Gold and Economic Freedom," 1966, 321Gold, http://www.321gold.com/fed/greenspan/1966.html. This article originally appeared in "The Objectivist" newsletter (1966), reprinted in Ayn Rand's "Capitalism: The Unknown Idea," (Signet, 1986).
[16] Ken Little, "What Stock Investors Should Know About Inflation," About, http://stocks.about.com/od/marketnews/a/Inflat101105.htm [accessed January 15, 2008].
[17] George D. Lambert, "Curbing the Effects of Inflation," Investopedia, http://www.investopedia.com/articles/05/061605.asp.

According to Ken Little, author of the article "What Stock Investors Should Know About Inflation," if you invest in fixed-rate bonds or CDs, you've already made a "bet" on inflation, whether you know it or not. That's because traditional fixed-rate investments don't always outpace inflation when you look at their real return to the investor. A clear example of the effects of inflation can be made when you consider that $10,000 in 1980 would only buy $3,998 in goods today.[18]

Many senior citizens who rely on CDs for retirement income end up going back to work because their liquid investments don't keep pace with inflation; nor do they offer any tax efficiency. Thus, these people usually have to spend their golden years working at fast food restaurants or retail stores, which, I'm sure, is not what they'd had in mind for retirement. If you doubt this, just examine your own financials with your advisor or tax preparer and see if the CD you've invested in is working as a superlative retirement tool.

So, what's the best way to combat inflation? The traditional approach is to broaden your horizons out of the dollar and into real property, commodities and foreign currencies, or something that gives you tax-free buildup. In other words, make investments in instruments with returns higher than the inflation rate and tax rates. This does not mean that you should invest in high-risk instruments.

You may think, after reading this chapter, that I'm against investing in the stock market. That isn't the case. I just believe that equity funds, for the most part, are not the best option for you. There are real opportunities for making money in the market, but I'm of the opinion that to garner real success, you would likely need something on the order of $2 million liquid to really take advantage of the premium opportunities in the market.

In Chapter Eleven, I'll reveal better opportunities that remain fairly liquid, and that offer tax reduction and growth to outpace inflation.

---

[18] Ken Little, "What Stock Investors Should Know About Inflation," About.com, http://stocks.about.com/od/marketnews/a/Inflat101105.htm [accessed January 30, 2008].

What We Learned

Most investors in mutual funds have no idea what they are invested in.

1. There are five separate fees that mutual funds charge:
    a. Management fees
    b. Brokerage commissions
    c. Sales loads
    d. Advertising costs
    e. Operating costs

2. The performance of equity funds from 1980 to 2005 as a measured return (S&P 500 Index) averaged 12.3 percent per year.

3. Only three equity funds out of a sample of 355 that started in 1970—just eight-tenths of one percent—survived or did well.

4. CDs offer no tax benefit and cannot outpace inflation.

It's fun to play around…it's human nature to try to select the right horse… [But] for the average person, I'm more of an indexer… The predictability is so high… For ten, fifteen, twenty years you'll be in the eighty-fifth percentile of performance. Why would you screw it up?
—Charles Schwab[19]

---

[19] Bogle, 59.

CHAPTER SEVEN

Wealth Pillar One: Leverage

The first pillar of wealth that we will discuss is leverage. This word has many possible definitions but in a financial sense, leverage means borrowing capital to increase the strength or size of an investment. This concept is attractive because it allows investors to invest large sums of money without risking a great deal of their own capital—essentially because leverage is the use of other people's money for your own investment purposes.

Leverage is one of the most powerful investment tools you can use to build wealth, but it is often misunderstood or underutilized by people who think it unwise to borrow money, no matter how harmless the venture. Leverage is used by most people at some point in their lives, most commonly to buy houses. If you don't have the cash to purchase a house outright, you can borrow capital and increase the return on your outlay through a mortgage.

Actually, most people consider a mortgage the only safe bet on leverage they'll make, unless they are in a subprime adjustable. There is a great deal of mistrust associated with borrowing money, yet people seem to overcome this fear when buying homes. People consider it normal and safe, because they're sure their homes will increase in value, because they plan on holding on to the investment for a long period of time and because they know how much they'll be paying to complete the purchase.

But as you're learning now, a home is not an investment in any real sense of the word. Unless you use the equity in the home to extend your wealth, a home is really a liability. That fact is becoming apparent to anyone who owns a home in one of the many depressed markets around the country.

How Most People Use Leverage

Let's look at a typical home purchase and see why so many people are willing to borrow the money to make it happen. Say you have $20,000 in cash but want to purchase a $300,000 house. With borrowed capital, or leverage, you can do just that, and by doing so you will give yourself access to a much larger investment return (you hope) than you could have with $20,000 alone.

The annual rate of appreciation on single-family homes has been approximately six percent per year. With an investment of $20,000 of your own money, you now have access to an investment return of $18,000 in the first year ($300,000 house x 1.06 = $318,000), assuming the home's appreciation stays close to the national historic average—which, as we've seen, doesn't always happen. The next year, the home could be worth $337,080. Again, these numbers are historic and not a predictor of the future.

In this scenario, you are essentially getting something of greater value than your own money can provide, and in a transaction that many people trust. But leverage is also an extremely powerful investment tool that goes beyond just purchasing a home, and is used in transactions as trusted as home-buying every day, by businesses and individuals alike. Leverage has been used for years to expand companies and enrich people's lives, and it keeps the world of real estate afloat. Leverage isn't something to fear; it's a tool of great power and one of the three pillars of wealth.

One of *Forbes*' 400 richest people in America is Gerald J. Ford—not to be confused with the late, former president Gerald Ford. This Ford made his fortune in banking, and is a self-made billionaire. His father ran a paint and body shop in Texas, and Ford lists his first job as working there with his father.

Ford purchased his first bank in 1975 at a cost of $1.2 million and later sold it for $80 million. He would eventually go on to be chairman of the board and CEO of Golden State Bancorp, Inc., which he sold, along with Ronald Perelman, to Citigroup for $6 billion in stock in 2002. Ford's other investments include AmeriCredit, Triad Financial and McMoRan Exploration.

When asked by *Forbes* to provide the best investment advice he'd ever received, Ford answered, "Leverage is a two-way street." This statement shows that he understands leverage, and that it can create enormous wealth. His statement also shows that leverage, like any financial tool, should be used with caution and an understanding of how it works.

Leverage Is a Common Financial Tool

Leverage is not a wild, risk-laden financial instrument used only by the extremely wealthy. In fact, it can be used by anyone to create wealth, though it does carry some risk because the investment is larger when leveraged, and therefore so is the potential for loss—hence Ford's reference to it being a two-way street. Businessmen like Ford look at borrowed capital as a means to a greater return.

One of the best-known leveraged-buyout practitioners is Nelson Peltz, who made his fortune by buying and selling large corporations using leverage, some of it in the form of junk bonds, with the help of Michael Milken. A leveraged buyout involves a private equity firm, like Peltz's Triarc, borrowing (or leveraging) against its own assets and the assets of a target company in order to raise the money necessary to buy a controlling share in the target company. The acquired company's cash flow is then used to pay off the debt, or the leveraged capital.

Through his two companies, Triarc and Trian, Peltz has been involved with Heinz, Snapple, Wendy's, Cadbury Schweppes and more, and has amassed a fortune of more than $1 billion. An example of the power of leverage can be seen in Peltz's purchase of Snapple from Quaker Oats in 1997 for $300 million; he later sold it to Cadbury Schweppes, in 2000, for $1.5 billion.

Though Ford and Peltz found their fortunes in banking and leveraged buyouts respectively, the most common use for leverage is in real estate, as we've discussed. You'll find more about using leverage in real estate in Chapter Ten.

The average person can use leverage to own several investment properties with little or no money down, and can then use the equity built on those properties to further build wealth. And, with the proper research and investment tools, those properties will carry less risk and will offer substantially greater rewards than investments made without leverage.

Using a home equity line of credit, or HELOC, is nothing new to many Americans. It's not uncommon to see people using equity loans to add additions to their homes or pay for a child's tuition, or even to cover medical bills and other expenses. But why waste your home's equity on items that don't offer substantial returns, or ones that actually depreciate? Using leverage well means using it for the advancement of your financial goals, not just to pay for physical items.

The idea behind a smart use of leverage is to increase your investment power. The equity you build in your home should be used for leveraged *investing*, not leveraged *spending*. With a few simple steps and some research, you can turn the leverage you already have access to—a HELOC—to build your position in investments that offer greater returns than the interest rate on the loan.

For example, if you had a low-interest mortgage of $180,000 on a home worth $270,000, you could take out a HELOC and invest it in an instrument that would return more than the simple interest on your HELOC—especially if you worked with a smart advisor who could guide you through the economics of finding tax-advantaged investment tools and arbitrage. The invested money, grown through compound interest, should far exceed the amount you pay back on the simple interest loan, and you've made the investment using leverage and arbitrage (which will be discussed further in the next chapter).

Though we've focused on real estate here, understand that leveraged investing, if done with care, can offer you investment power far beyond the cash you could possibly save for the same purpose. Some of the country's largest and most successful companies use leverage on a daily basis, and not just in the scope of borrowing money. They leverage their positions in the market, or they leverage their brands to expand business.

In addition, many insurance companies leverage themselves against fluctuations in the market by using put calls and options on the index, to take advantage of the arbitrage opportunities. The return on those transactions is often used to support the payouts on their indexed investment products.

There are also opportunities to use leverage to purchase a large insurance policy, which can create liquidity in an estate that has illiquid assets or needs liquid funding to pay potential estate taxes. Using a loan to an irrevocable trust, you can fund the purchase of an interest-bearing life insurance policy. With this tool, you can build wealth while avoiding some of the tax pitfalls associated with estate taxation.

More of this will be discussed in Chapter Eleven, but for now, know that succession capital can be built using leverage. It's just one of the many areas where leverage can help you earn a greater return on your investments.

That is not to say that all investments should be made with leverage, or that it's wise to borrow money when you're already heavily in debt. In fact, during the day-trading craze of the late 1990s, when many traders were using margin accounts—which were supported by money borrowed from the brokers—some found themselves in deeper trouble than they were prepared for when Internet stocks took a dive. The day traders saw margin accounts as a way to leverage purchasing power in a booming market. But, that borrowed money had to be paid back, just as it does in any leveraged investment.

Don't Fear Debt

Because of incidents like the dot-com bust and the high-interest debt many Americans carry around like anchors, people assume that debt is to be feared. But it would be a mistake to assume that all debt is bad.

Businesses have been using leverage to increase their purchasing power since the beginning of commerce, and it has become an accepted means of expanding potential investment returns. The principal here is that if an investment will return a certain amount of money over time, and you're fairly certain of the return, as you could be with a home, then isn't it better to invest more upfront than you could with your own available cash?

The answer is usually "yes," especially because of compound interest. The money you borrow—against your home, for example—will be tied to a fixed interest rate, so you know how much you'll need to pay back over the life of the loan. The interest on your investment, though, will compound over time.

If you took a home equity loan that had a six-percent interest rate on it, and invested it in an instrument that returned eight percent compounded over time, you would have successfully leveraged your assets into strong profits.

Maybe the best-known user of leverage in real estate is Donald Trump. He has often been criticized for his overuse of leverage, but his success at building his brand can't be denied. Trump knows how to leverage more than just the real property he owns; he has leveraged his brand and has used its power to draw investors to his projects and a strong customer base to his properties.

Trump's greatest success was probably the Trump Tower, located on the northeast corner of 56th Street and Fifth Avenue in New York City. The tower was built using financing from Chase Manhattan Bank; the Equitable Life Assurance Society of the United States owned the property and helped obtain the financing.

Trump Tower was completed in 1983 at an estimated cost of $201 million. The partnership kept the rights to the retail and office space, and Trump was able to buy out Equitable in 1986. It's estimated that by then, out of 268 condominium apartments in the tower, 251 of them had been sold for a total cost of $277 million. And, Trump had done it all with other people's money. He went on to become a master of leveraging his brand and his assets to increase profits.

For business owners, leverage provides a chance to prepare a powerful exit strategy. By leveraging your assets and even your accounts receivable, you can capture the power of your equity and take advantage of investment opportunities. It's a way to make your money work for you as you operate your business, and it ensures a healthy investment portfolio for when you decide to leave the business.

Don't just assume you'll have a nest egg from the sale of a business—it might not be worth anything when you decide to get out. I know from my work with business owners that you should use the power of your assets while you have them, and I've assisted numerous owners in creating predictable and profitable exits from their businesses.

In today's economy, with its questions about the strength of Social Security and our employers' abilities to secure our futures, even older investors are looking toward leverage as a way to earn greater security. The once-unthought-of notion of risking your assets near retirement age has now become a consideration for many baby boomers. Instruments like leveraged ETFs (exchange-traded funds) are now available for people who are unwilling to sit back on risk-free portfolios. (More about estate planning will be discussed in Chapter Sixteen).

A word of caution about leverage: Increased investment power means increased risk. The more you put into an investment vehicle, the more you have to lose. You must assume risk with all investments, and using leverage should be done with caution and the advice of an experienced financial advisor. Used properly, it is one of the three pillars of wealth.

What We Learned

1. Leverage is the use of borrowed capital to increase the size or strength of an investment position.

2. Leverage is used by the average person to purchase a home or car.

3. Leverage can be used to go beyond the mere acquisition of a home. Used properly, it can help create a strong investment portfolio that takes advantage of the power of compound interest.

4. Leverage comes with risk and should be used only after careful consideration and advisement by a financial advisor, who can provide you with the advantage of depth of understanding and experience.

CHAPTER EIGHT

Wealth Pillar Two: Arbitrage

The second secret pillar of wealth is arbitrage, which is the act of simultaneously purchasing and selling an asset in order to profit from a difference in pricing in two or more separate markets. This usually takes place on different exchanges or marketplaces and is also known as "riskless profit," because it doesn't involve negative cash flow.

To make it simpler, let's look at an example: If stuffed animals sell for $3 apiece in Cleveland, and they sell for $7 apiece in Cincinnati, you could purchase them in Cleveland and sell them in Cincinnati for a tidy $4 profit. This represents an arbitrage profit.

Of course, this example is an oversimplification of the process and doesn't take into account the nuances of arbitrage and the power it holds for you in building your wealth. But the idea of arbitrage—the use of varying price points—is what we want to focus on.

Arbitrage is possible when one of three conditions is met:

1. The law of one price is not in effect. In other words, an asset isn't priced the same on all markets.

2. Two assets that generate the same cash flows are not going for the same price. This would be like two business owners who both make the same from their businesses selling those businesses for different prices.

3. An asset with a known future price is selling for less money today. This one can get complex but it basically has to do with knowing that something will gain value and purchasing now will take advantage of that increase.

Here's another example, to help clarify: You take out a refinance loan on real property (something like your house) at 7.5 percent interest and invest it in a tax-free environment at an eight-percent return rate. The question is, does the half-percent profit on the surface warrant the transaction?

Let's look a layer deeper in the transaction. If your borrowed money is related to real estate, you generally get a tax deduction on the interest; depending on your tax bracket, it should be at least 2.5 percent. You'll also get help from inflation, since the amount of money you owe is set and its value will decrease over time. In other words, if you owe $200 a month, over time, the burden will seem smaller as $200 becomes less valuable.

Because of the dual effect of inflation and tax deduction, we now have a reduction of 4.5 percent in the 7.5 percent that was borrowed. Consequently, our eight-percent return is effectively costing us only three percent in interest on our property loan. Now, the 7.5 percent you borrowed is receiving an arbitrage of five percent on the upside. However, this is not the end. When you deploy the funds into a tax-free situation, it receives a triple compound on the interest, in a way, because you're receiving compound interest on your money, plus interest on the money that would have gone to taxes. The three percent that you borrowed from the real estate is simple interest and never changes, while your invested dollars receive the triple compound. After several years, the result is staggering. Albert Einstein was rumored to have said "The most powerful force in the universe is compound interest." Whether he did or not, the phrase is spot on.

I've seen many clients do this with home equity and deploy it into investment-grade life insurance products, which are not designed solely for the death benefit; they also create an unmatched place to compound your money free of tax. When you want to tap into the funds, you can characterize the draw as a loan and further avoid the taxes. I'll explain this concept in more depth later in the book.

Professional arbitragers usually make their transactions on different exchanges or markets, using simultaneous transactions, but we're not going to focus on those high-level transactions. Instead, I want you to look at arbitrage as your ability to find markets or investment tools wherein your money is more powerful than in comparable markets. Professional arbitragers are usually equipped with sophisticated equipment that allows them to make simultaneous transactions in multiple markets; you need to learn how to take advantage of arbitrage using your own investment tools.

Arbitrage Opportunities

For your purposes, we'll focus on the arbitrage opportunities in tax-deferred or tax-free, interest-bearing asset classes, such as life insurance umbrellas. For you, arbitrage will become your ability to find the varying rates of return you can secure with your money while playing the differences to build your wealth.

A classic example of an arbitrage opportunity—in the sense that we're using it—lies in the way we pay our mortgages. If you're like many homeowners, whose parents taught them that all debt is bad and that mortgages are albatrosses to be cast off as soon as possible, you're probably trying to pay off your mortgage early. You're thinking that the sooner you get rid of your mortgage, the sooner you can cushion your retirement nest egg with all of that loose money.

But here's an important lesson all wealthy people understand: No one ever got rich just by saving money. Or, put another way, paying off debt is not the same as accumulating assets. I stress this because many people think they will be better off financially if they eliminate their mortgages, but that's not automatically correct. Despite the fact that millions of Americans believe it to be true doesn't make it so. Many of you have been ill advised, and you need to know why.

Let's look at the arbitrage opportunities available for that very same money. The money you use to pay off your mortgage comes from your income and has already been taxed. If you pay off an extra $1,000 of your mortgage, you probably had to earn $1,250 or more to do so. But can the money you use to pay off your mortgage be more powerful in another market and offer you a better return in the long run? The answer is "yes!"

For example, if you're working for a company that offers a 401(k), and especially if it offers matching contributions, you have an opportunity to arbitrage your earnings. Think about this: The money you put into your 401(k) is tax deferred, which means that all of your earnings go into the investment, instead of just what's left after taxes. Also, if your company offers matched assets, you're getting something for nothing. Your money becomes even more powerful in the 401(k) "market" than in the mortgage payoff "market" that we're using in our example.

If you choose to invest in the 401(k) instead of paying extra toward your mortgage, you can use the entire $1,250 you earned, plus the money your employer provides, to earn for your retirement. Over the life of your mortgage, your money is worth more in your 401(k) or another tax-sheltered investment such as an interest-bearing life insurance policy.

This is just one example of the arbitrage opportunities you can use to maximize the power of your money. In general, 401(k)s don't offer the kind of returns we're looking for because they are, in essence, mutual funds, which don't generally perform as they should. When you factor in the fees these funds charge—two to three percent disclosed, plus an additional one percent undisclosed—you're not getting the advantages we want in an investment. Plus, when you open the 401(k) after retirement, the income is taxed as normal income. Soon enough, you'll realize how little it all amounts to.

We need to think bigger and more proactively when creating wealth for ourselves, and that's where arbitrage comes in.

Many of the opportunities we'll discuss will be related to the life insurance vehicles many of us already have, such as the above example.

For now, we'll give a general overview of some of the opportunities available to us. For more detail, see chapters ten and eleven.

How Powerful Is Arbitrage?

George Kaiser, the twenty-sixth richest American according to *Forbes* magazine, was asked by the publication about the best investment advice he'd ever heard. His answer was an indication of how powerful the concept of arbitrage is, and how it goes beyond simple buying and selling.

Kaiser told *Forbes*, "First, understand the conventional wisdom, and then carefully articulate to yourself where it is in error and arbitrage the difference."[20]

Kaiser's words of wisdom hold true in the example above, and they've helped bring him great wealth. Understanding the conventional wisdom, whether it be about mortgages, as in our example, or about banking and natural gas in Kaiser's case, helps us see areas wherein it is sometimes wrong. In the case of mortgages, we see that the "pay it off as early as possible" mantra of old doesn't always hold true today.

Kaiser took over his family's oil and gas business in 1969. He expanded the company into real estate, banking and derivatives, and made a fortune in the process. He now owns 45 million shares of BOK Financial and runs Excelerate Energy. Kaiser also helps fight childhood poverty through the George Kaiser Family Foundation.[21]

What Kaiser understands, and what we're trying to learn, is that arbitrage holds great power because it takes advantage of pre-existing market conditions and doesn't involve a great deal of development to generate a profit. Arbitragers are fond of calling arbitrage "riskless investing" because of this.

What to Look For

One of the most important considerations to make when searching for arbitrage opportunities is the tax implications of your

---

[20] "The 400 Richest Americans: The Entrepreneurs." Forbes.com Sept. 21, 2006 http://www.forbes.com/entrepreneurs/2006/09/20/ent-manage_biz_06rich400_self_made_entrepreneurs_george_kaiser.html [accessed Jan. 25, 2008].
[21] Matthew Miller, ed., "The Forbes 400," Forbes (September 20, 2007), http://www.forbes.com/lists/2007/54/richlist07_George-Kaiser_OXNB_print.html (accessed Oct. 2, 2007).

investments. Tax-deferred asset classes, such as real estate and life insurance, offer opportunities to use more of your money, just as your 401(k) does.

When we take advantage of tax-free, interest-bearing investment tools, such as life insurance policies or tax-free bonds (if the rates are favorable), we are essentially earning triple-compound interest on our money. We have the compound interest from the investment vehicle and we are avoiding the biggest hurdle to earnings: taxes.

Home Equity Loan

One of the most powerful tools you can use to arbitrage and leverage your way to wealth is managing your home equity. A home equity loan or line of credit is obtained by offering the equity in your home as collateral for a cash loan. If you put $20,000 down on your home, then the day you purchase your home, you have $20,000 in equity. Five years down the road, your equity will be comprised of any money you've paid toward the mortgage, plus any appreciation in your home.

Arbitraging your home equity involves playing the differences between the simple interest you'd pay on a home equity loan and the return on investments you could make that would take advantage of compound interest or offer a greater return than the debt service on your loan.

Arbitraging With Life Insurance

One of the most powerful tools you can use is a tax-free life insurance policy. Many policies offer smaller fees than mutual funds and unlike mutual funds, life insurance policies create tax-free distribution capabilities.

Arbitraging your money involves using a home equity loan, borrowed at simple interest, to invest in a life insurance policy that earns compound interest. It also involves a little patience. Even if your life insurance policy bears only a five-percent return annually and your simple interest on the equity loan is also five percent, you'll still come out ahead over time, if you allow compound interest to take effect.

In addition, you can overfund your policy beyond the death benefit in order to maximize your investment outcome. The result is a powerful investment tool that uses arbitrage to maximize earnings on money you've already got sitting around.

Here's an example: Julie has $100,000 in equity in her home. She decides to arbitrage her money in order to maximize her wealth for retirement. So, she borrows $50,000 at five-percent interest against her home. She puts the $50,000 into a life insurance policy that returns five percent compounded annually, tax-free. In her first year, Julie breaks even. But in the second year, her money in the life insurance policy will earn an extra $2,625 on top of the five percent she owes on her home equity debt service.

The beauty of the life insurance policy is that even when you take money out of it, thus cashing in on your investment, you can do so as a tax-free loan to yourself. The power of the policy only grows with time; for example, in a decade (assuming an annual five-percent return compounded over ten years), Julie will have $81,444 in her life insurance policy against which to draw. A portion of that—$31,444, to be exact—will be interest alone and will not affect her death benefit.

However, this example is a simple one and doesn't take into account the individual situations we all face. like our eligibility for life insurance, the premiums we might to pay, etc. To get a more personalized projection, I encourage each of my clients to have a professional run their numbers, to find the best vehicle for taking advantage of arbitrage. But, the idea here is clear: You have at your fingertips opportunities to earn more on your money, if you know which markets will benefit you the most.

By examining the earning power of our dollars, both in a mortgage and in a tax-free life insurance policy, we've seen that we can earn more by sheltering our money from taxes and taking advantage of compound interest. The appreciation on your home isn't guaranteed, and it certainly doesn't compound. Why not have your money where it will do you the most good?

Knowing Your Investment Tools

Arbitraging successfully means knowing what you're invested in, because arbitrage is time sensitive. You'll need to take advantage of interest rates and rates of return while they benefit you, and for that, you'll need the help of a knowledgeable advisor.

I've seen many life insurance brokers who didn't even know the internal rate of return on the policies they were selling, and so they set people up in the wrong vehicles at the wrong times.

Why You Need Arbitrage and Leverage

Achieving comfort in retirement is going to take a great deal more than a simple 401(k). You're going to need to set up a series of tools that maximize your earning potential; leverage and arbitrage offer you two of the principles you need to get going.

Arbitrage is a wonderful tool because you can use it alongside your 401(k) and mortgage. It's a good supplement that can earn you money based solely on the differing rates of return in investment tools already available to you. Many of you already have a life insurance policy—meaning that you're sitting on an arbitraging opportunity and you probably don't even know it.

Look at what you've got. Seek out professional advice and start arbitraging your way to better returns.

Use Caution

Arbitrage is like any other financial tool in that it should be used with caution and only after you've run the numbers. Everybody's situation is unique and I always do a thorough analysis of a client's portfolio before I start making moves.

It's important to understand that investments carry risk—even the "riskless" arbitrage we're looking to take advantage of. The strategies we've discussed are only for individuals looking for investment opportunities; others may feel more comfortable paying off their mortgages early instead. That's also fine. I've seen people pay off their mortgages in fifteen years with no dramatic change in lifestyle or cash flow. However, they also see no increases in their retirement savings, either.

What We Learned

1. Arbitrage is one of the Three Secret Pillars of Wealth; by using them carefully, you can create great wealth with the tools and markets already in your possession.

2. Wealthy people like George Kaiser understand that successful arbitrage takes advantage of disparities in the conventional wisdom.

3. Investment vehicles like tax-free, interest-bearing life insurance policies offer a better "market" for your money and therefore present opportunities for arbitrage.

4. Arbitrage can be used with leverage and cash flow to create great wealth.

CHAPTER NINE

Wealth Pillar Three: Cash Flow

We've all heard the expression "cash is king." Well, that happens to be true. Cash flow is critical to success in business and wealth building, and is one of the most important indicators of financial health for both businesses and individuals.

Cash flow tells us how much we're spending and how much we're making, and though it isn't the only financial indicator we should pay attention to, it certainly says a lot about the health of our businesses' and families' finances. If you want control over your finances, you need to understand how your cash flow works.

Cash flow is important because it is critical to staying solvent. Cash pays for daily expenses like milk and bread and your mortgage. Your cash outlay, measured against how much you bring in, is a good indicator of how healthy your finances are because if you want to stay above water, you need to have positive net-cash flow.

As an example, let's look at a typical family. If they own a home and two cars, they have assets and some net worth. But if they lose cash flow through unexpected expenses or the loss of a job, they'll have no cash to pay for food, heating or their mortgage. They're going to be in trouble because the equity in their house isn't going to pay their bills—hence the expression "cash is king."

Now, before you go thinking that this family could simply pay for needed expenses with credit cards or a home equity line of credit, just remember that securing credit requires incoming cash. Without it, securing emergency funds may be impossible.

Without cash, commerce would come to a halt—unless, of course, we all wanted to go back to bartering. Without cash, you wouldn't be able to buy the things you wanted or needed, and you would certainly have a difficult time investing.

But despite its importance, most people aren't even aware of the precise numbers related to their cash flow. If you were asked to name exactly how much cash you earn on a monthly basis, and how much exactly you spend, I know some of you would stumble while trying answer. This is because we frequently spend $20 here and $20 there without thinking about it; we only think about it at the end of the month, when we're out of money and can't figure out why.

Because your cash flow is crucial, it never hurts to set up a chart that logs how much you take in—from your job, investments or loans—and how much you spend on anything, no matter how insignificant.

What Cash Flow Says About You

Cash flow is so important to businesses that many consider it vital to valuing a company's viability. The same holds true for your situation. An increasing or stable cash flow means that a company will likely be able to meet its cash needs, which is vital to healthy operations. Companies have bills, too, just like we do, and if they aren't paid, the whole thing could go under—even if it's making an operating profit.

When you buy stock in a company, you are essentially buying a stake in the future cash earnings of the company. Cash is how companies pay out dividends, expand into new markets and buy back stocks.[22] Doesn't it make sense to secure the future of your own finances so that you're guaranteed returns? It's what you ask for from companies you invest in, so it should be something you ask of yourself.

The significance of cash flow to businesses is mirrored by the importance of cash flow to the individual. You already know that you need cash to pay bills, but you also need it to expand your

---

[22] Paul Tracy, "The Importance of Cash Flow," Street Authority (March 24, 2005), http://www.streetauthority.com/cmnts/pt/2005/03-24.asp [accessed Oct. 11, 2007].

wealth and invest in your future. Cash holdings allow you to seize opportunities for expansion of your own operations, and they help keep you solvent. They also help you weather emergencies, when cash is needed for repairs to your home, or for medical bills.

The Categories of Cash Flow

Cash flow is usually broken down into three categories:

1. **Operational cash flow**: Cash you bring in from your principal source of income; this is probably your everyday job.

2. **Investment cash flow**: Money you spend to acquire an investment, or that you earn from an investment.

3. **Financing cash flow**: Money you spend to pay off loans or money you receive as the result of a loan.[23]

You can look at these classifications in your own financial operations. Operational cash flow can be seen as cash you receive as payment from your job, and the money you spend on daily expenses like food, gas and mortgage payments.

Investment cash flow is the same for you as it is for a company: It's money you earn or lose through the investment vehicles you choose for yourself. If you have money in stocks, real estate or the life insurance vehicles we've discussed, then any cash earnings you take away from those will be considered investment cash flow.

Financing cash ties into the discussions we've already had about leverage and arbitrage. The home equity loans and lines of credit we've discussed using for other investment vehicles would be considered financing cash flows. As we've seen, financing cash flow, like other cash flows, can be both negative and positive. Your goal, of course, will be to make your cash flow return a net positive. And remember, because mortgages are debt vehicles that rely on your

---

[23] Wikipedia contributors, "Cash Flow," Wikipedia, The Free Encyclopedia, http://en.wikipedia.org/wiki/Cash_flow [accessed October 11, 2007].

ability to pay them pack, you have to have cash flow to secure a refinance or home equity line of credit.

As an example, let's look at one client I had, who was diagnosed with cancer in his twenties. He was unable to secure a home equity line of credit to help cover his expenses because he was unable to work. I've also seen the same sort of thing happen to hurricane victims. They had equity in their homes but very little cash flow, and once their homes were gone, they had to rely on insurance payments, some of which took years to receive.

When we invest, the goal is always to create positive cash flow in addition to the appreciation on our investments. What's the point of investing in something if it isn't going to help fund further investments, or help you buy the things you need or want in retirement? Once you've stopped working, you're going to need cash flow to help pay your everyday bills and other expenses that you can't foresee but should prepare for. You'll need cash to maintain a comfortable lifestyle. You don't want to work for thirty years and build a solid lifestyle only to lose it all when you stop working. In order to avoid that, you'll need cash.

That's why it's so important to turn equity into cash while your home is still in one piece. You need to turn that liability into an asset. Most people simply pay their mortgages and fail to use them for generating positive returns outside of the appreciation on their homes. Keep in mind that your home's value is not tied to how much you owe on it, so using the equity in it to generate further earnings is a smart play.

Remember, negative cash flow—money you're sending out the door—is negative only in the sense that it's marked as a deduction on your ledger, not in the sense that it's *bad*. "Negative" just means that cash has gone out of your coffers and been put toward an expense or investment. Also remember that you do want to make sure that your net cash flow is positive, and that your negative cash flow is going toward investments that will eventually return positive cash flow.

This means that you have to think about where your money is going. There are the necessary items: cars, homes, schooling, food.

But there are surely items that are either unnecessary or that you pay too much for. Is your cash going toward things that are necessary? Is your cash going toward things that will eventually return cash flow to you? If the answer to these questions is currently "no," then you need to view your finances the way a company would: as though they are in trouble.

The Blockbuster Man

Wayne Huizenga, owner of the NFL's Miami Dolphins and the driving force behind two billion-dollar companies, once told *Fortune* magazine that the best investment advice he'd ever heard was "cash flow."

Huizenga founded Waste Management, Inc. after buying a used garbage truck in 1962. He would eventually buy 133 other hauling companies before taking Waste Management public in 1972. By 1983, his was the largest hauler in the United States, and Huizenga sold his stake in the company in 1984; three years later, he invested in a fledgling video rental chain called Blockbuster. He would sell his stake in Blockbuster seven years later for $8.4 billion.[24]

Huizenga has found success in multiple industries, his latest venture being AutoNation, a network of car dealerships that's become a *Fortune* 500 company like his others. Like other successful businessmen and women, Huizenga understands that cash flow is what makes the world go 'round. Without cash, his businesses wouldn't have been able to make acquisitions or expansions, and though he may have been rich in assets, cash is what allowed Huizenga to build his fortune—which is estimated at $2.5 billion by *Forbes* magazine.

Cash Flow Vehicles

A cash flow vehicle could be almost any investment that returns cash. But, since we've been focusing on life insurance vehicles and real estate, let's look at some of the opportunities in these areas that you can use to earn yourself some cash flow.

---

[24] Matthew Miller, ed., "The Forbes 400," Forbes (September 20, 2007), http://www.forbes.com/lists/2007/54/richlist07_H-Wayne-Huizenga_E353.html [accessed Oct. 15, 2007].

Real estate purchases, whether rental properties or your own home, should be looked at as ways to further your cash flow, leverage and arbitrage opportunities. If you purchase a property for the sake of investment, then be sure you're getting a return. Cash flow from a property will ensure that you have enough to cover repairs, vacancies or other emergencies. Remember, equity isn't going to do you any good if your home no longer exists, such as after a fire, hurricane or severe flood. Equity should be used for cash flow, whether the operational kind or the financing kind.

When you examine a prospective investment opportunity in real estate, you have to ask yourself important questions about the potential earning power of the property. Do your homework on similar rental properties in the area and understand the math before you commit money to the project. Does the property make financial sense? Purchases like these should not be made on a whim, or based on emotion. Instead, ask yourself, "Will the property earn me cash?"

Your other vehicle of choice is tax-free life insurance, which will also net you cash flow when you need it the most: in retirement. The tax-free compound interest you earn from your life insurance vehicle is going to afford you a steady stream of cash flow once it's had time to mature. And, the great thing about the cash flow is that it comes in the form of tax-free loans to yourself, from the death benefit. That's a huge advantage over other investment forms such as 401(k)s and mutual funds, which are subject to income and capital gains when the money is withdrawn.

Remember, the whole reason to make investments toward your retirement or toward expanding your wealth in general is to create the cash you want or need for expenses and luxuries. If your goal is to own a large home and live in luxury, then you would do well to have a plan that will afford you the cash flow you'll need.

For most people, however, cash flow goals will be grounded in the realization that retirement will be costly, expressly because the cash flow will have diminished. Your investments should be organized to help generate the cash flow you'll need once you've stopped working. The cessation of an everyday job will represent the greatest dip in cash flow many of us will experience, whether it be through retirement or the loss of a job. We must be prepared for these eventualities with supplemental cash flow.

As with any investments or financial maneuverings, caution should be the bedrock in how you handle your money. Create a cash flow chart that shows exactly how much money you are earning, how much you are spending, and how much you hope to create in net cash flow. By setting realistic cash flow goals, you'll know exactly how much you need to meet your ambitions, and planning will be that much easier.

Cash Flow in Real Estate Investments

Cash flow is the true lifeblood of any real estate transaction, but it is sometimes overlooked by the novice. It should not be secondary in your examination of a deal. Many real estate dealers promote the tax benefits of a deal but not the cash flow because of the changing tides in the mortgage industry. I think it's important to adhere to the idea that you're investing to create cash flow, which means that you should wait until you find a deal that will give it to you.

In what I consider one of the best books on cash flow, *What Every Real Estate Investor Needs to Know About Cash Flow*, Frank Gallinelli provides a pretty good rule of thumb. To paraphrase: Don't make a decision to buy, hold or sell based on emotion. Instead, base your decisions on the promise of cash flow. Don't settle for anything less than the cash flow you want from a deal.[25]

Now, sometimes an investment will start out creating positive cash flow and then go negative due to market conditions. Regardless, you should, at the outset, make your goal generating cash flow—the exception being a deal that has high potential to generate cash flow in the future. This, though, is gambling, and a craps table may give you the same odds. Where there is negative cash flow in a property, there will be reduced lifestyle cash flow, and that's no fun.

---

[25] Frank Gallinelli, What Every Real Estate Investor Needs to Know About Cash Flow (NY: McGraw-Hill, 2003), 14.

I could drone on at length about this point, but I won't. Instead, I will highly recommend that all serious investors put the Frank Gallinelli book on their reading lists, so that they can learn about how cash flow works relative to real estate. Another great book that should be on either a seasoned or neophyte real estate investor's bookshelf is Robert Campbell's *Timing the Real Estate Market*.

What We Learned

1. Cash flow is the measure of how much cash you take in and expend.

2. Cash flow can be either negative or positive, in the form of expenditures or income from any number of sources.

3. Cash flow is crucial to running a business or being successful in building wealth.

4. Cash flow falls into three categories: operational cash flow from working or business operations; investment cash flow; and financing cash flow, which comes from loans, either into or out of your coffers.

5. Cash flow should be your main goal in your investment plan. Without cash flow, your expenses will not be met and your retirement will be considerably reduced compared to the lifestyle to which you're accustomed.

CHAPTER TEN

Real Estate

Don't wait to buy land, buy land and wait!
—Will Rogers

Real estate investing is exciting not only because it involves using the pillar of leverage, but also because ordinary people can create incredible wealth in a short time with it. I know, because I've seen it happen.

It's also exciting because there are always opportunities to make strong returns, regardless of how the market is doing. But, like other forms of investment, real estate investing takes discipline, education and smart decision making to be successful. I've met with clients who've made impulse purchases and the results were usually disastrous. You'll learn more about the possible pitfalls of real estate investment in Chapter Seventeen, but for now, let's look at a little bit of its history, and at the options you have in today's market.

A Brief History of Land Ownership

Land ownership has long been considered a sign of true wealth. In ancient India, a person was said to be wealthy if he owned land and livestock. [26] Throughout history, land ownership has assumed many forms and there are many theories about why people have been so eager to expand their ownership of land. Two prominent

---

[26] P.M. Tamboli and Y.L. Nene, "Science in India with Special Reference to Agriculture," Asian Agri-History Foundation,
http://www.agrihistory.org/Science%20in%20India%20with%20Special%20Reference%20to%20Agriculture.pdf [accessed January 15, 2008].

schools of thought on the matter seem to stand out. According to B.D. Roberts, "…land represents hunger—the desire to secure sufficient land for one's existence." Roberts also contends that land represents "the lust for power expressed through control of land and, consequently, its inhabitants." [27]

The early history of England demonstrates these trends in its use of feudalism, a system that granted all lands to a king and his vassals. The vassals pledged their loyalty to the king in return for land, and they, in turn, were in charge of their own vassals, the peasants. [28]

More recent history, up to and including the last couple of years, has seen property ownership at an all-time high, with historical lows in the interest rates for financing real property. Even now, as we move into what looks like a recession, real property still appears to represent the best opportunity for wealth creation, and is still creating the most millionaires and billionaires the world over. There is no other asset you can purchase with nothing down, or very little down through leverage, while earning a potentially infinite return.

According to Frank Gallinelli, "Return on investment, by its simplest definition, is the amount of the return divided by the amount of the investment. Anything divided by zero is infinity. Hence, even a one-cent return on a zero-dollar investment would be an infinite rate of return." [29] There are few investment opportunities that offer that kind of turnaround and fewer still that offer real opportunities in even the worst markets.

By educating yourself about the opportunities available to you, you can learn to make quick, insightful decisions. In retirement planning, that's a huge asset, because time is always against you.

There are at least eight reasons why deals are always available, no matter what the real estate market is doing. There is no magic

---

[27] B.D. Roberts, "Tenure in Pre-Norman England," The School of Cooperative Individualism, http://www.cooperativeindividualism.org/roberts-b-d_land-tenure-pre-norman-england.html (reprinted from The Freeman, February 1939)
[28] Roberts, http://www.cooperativeindividualism.org/roberts-b-d_land-tenure-pre-norman-england.
[29] Frank Gallinelli, "Rate of Return on No Money Down (and Other Tales from the Deep Woods)," Real Data, http://www.realdata.com/ls/rateofreturn.shtml.

here—just human circumstances that create opportunities, if you know how to look for them. The eight reasons are:

1. Divorce
2. Job loss
3. Job relocation
4. Bankruptcy
5. Health problems
6. Estate inheritance/probate
7. Out-of-town owners
8. TMTF

If you're wondering what TMTF is, it stands for "too much too fast," and it's what happens during a peaky real estate market or any buyer's market where people are buying at retail rather than looking for a great price. This is what happened during the recent real estate craze, when people rushed in to buy second properties, ignoring the numbers and buying at top-of-the-market prices. They didn't consider what their exit strategies would be, nor did they plan on how to overcome an unexpected shift in the market.

Therefore, these unfortunate investors created a great opportunity for others to buy property at a discount. The wise investors looked for undervalued properties during the buying craze and are now better off than most.

In a 2006 *CNN Money* report, certain areas of the country were declared to be undervalued. In fact, dozens of areas were found to have real estate selling for well below market value. I don't know about you, but these are the areas I would have been looking at when the novice investors were inflating areas like California, Arizona, Las Vegas and Florida.

Think of these areas as akin to the stocks whose share prices in 2000 were relative to the P/E (price to earnings) ratio and represented opportunities for growth. In that sense, the "multiple" paid for real estate in certain areas of the country back then was not sustainable and while some areas skyrocketed overnight, they plunged just as fast.[30] At the time of this book's printing, many of these areas were on the rise, with developments moving in.

The Importance of Real Estate

There are numerous strategies for making money in real estate, and I'll name and explain some of the most prominent ones in this chapter. At the end of the day, however, there is no replacement for a good education.

Your education should enable you to carry out due diligence and take a solid look at the numbers. Salespeople lie, but math does not, and I recommend that you get a good spreadsheet or software program to run all the numbers associated with an investment property, including your debt service (mortgage), housing association fees, taxes and so on. Such programs can also help determine how much rent you might fetch in the area. When trying to determine what a realistic rent is in the area you're considering, a good Website to check is Rent-O-Meter at http://www.rentometer.com/.

Statistics show that most of the real estate investment plans purchased from companies advertising on television do not create a volume of successful investors. Purchasing these systems is a little like being the kid who buys a book about karate, hoping to learn how to do it by looking at the pictures. The kid who actually pays his dues in a master's dojo will learn quicker and with more depth, and it's the same for real estate investors: You have to get involved to really learn the game. At the printing of this book, there is at least one real estate investing university that is dedicated to teaching the subject with a full lesson plan, like a college course, rather than through the seminar approach.

There is also the Robert Kiyosaki series of books and seminars, *Rich Dad, Poor Dad.* I think Robert has done and continues to do a great job in both motivating and educating people on the pitfalls of just standing still and not taking action. He also shows readers

---

[30] Les Christie, "Most Overvalued Housing Markets," CNNMoney.com (January 3, 2006), http://money.cnn.com/2006/01/23/real_estate/most_markets_more_overpriced/index.htm [accessed January 15, 2008].

how to move from being employees or stuck in their own businesses to developing passive income, which real estate sometimes represents.

Real Estate Investment Strategies

The mainstream strategies offering investors the most money are the tried and true buy and hold (like a stock), fix and flip, rehab, wholesale property and distressed property investing (foreclosure, short sale and REO). I have personally made money with these strategies and I'm of the opinion that you make your money when you buy the property, and that selling is just a byproduct of that great purchase.

By that, I mean that the research and work you do prior to the purchase is where the real difference is made. You shouldn't be figuring out how you're going to make money on the property after you've already purchased it. For this reason, I've moved to the very simple strategy of buying and holding at least for a couple of years.

Since there is a lot about foreclosures in the newspapers and on the news at the moment, let's start with this strategy as our first real estate investing tactic for wealth. If done right, purchasing foreclosed properties is like finding a gold vein in a cave; if done incorrectly, it's a little like having the cavern collapse on you.

Distressed Property Techniques

Foreclosure: A foreclosure property is a home where a notice of default has been filed in the public records for non-payment of the mortgage, and a lender has given notice that unless the payments are brought up to date, the property will be sold to the highest bidder. Lenders can foreclose for other reasons, but the most common reason is the borrower being at least two payments in arrears. However, available equity may play a role in how soon a lender takes action and how negotiable he or she is.

Do you think lenders are more negotiable when there is a lot of equity in the home or when there is a little equity in the home? If you guessed the latter, you are correct. A lender is typically more agreeable to working out payments if there is little equity in the home, because then, they may have to short sell the property (discussed below).

Investors who specialize in buying foreclosures often prefer purchasing these homes before the foreclosure proceedings are final. Before approaching a seller in distress, consider that procedures vary from state to state, with most states offering protections to the homeowner. This means that most of them can stay on the property for up to a year during foreclosure proceedings, and that they have a chance to pay the money they owe in order to retain the property.

Also, you'll likely have to provide notices about any equity purchases to the homeowners; if you don't, you can face fines and other problems. And, finally, remember what a foreclosure really means. You're kicking someone out on the street, and you need to be prepared to face that reality when you get involved in this kind of transaction.

States have varying laws governing foreclosures and some follow California law. To completely understand your rights as a foreclosure buyer, contact a local real estate lawyer. There are some limitations placed on real estate agents when representing an investor, so make sure you check the laws in your state. California prohibits an agent from representing a buyer when certain conditions exist, such as if the buyer does not intend to occupy the property and the home is the seller's primary residence. In those cases, bonds usually have to be secured and California doesn't yet offer that option. [31]

In addition to local laws, you're required to abide by the Home Equity Sales Act. This grants the seller certain rights when it comes to rescinding a deal, and failure to notify the seller of their rights could grant them the right to take the property back well after the sale.

Make sure you a consult a real estate attorney before getting involved in foreclosed properties. It's a lot more complex than some people let on, and doing it wrong could lead to major trouble. [32]

---

[31] Dorene Shirley, "The Real Estate Connection," Campbell Express (May, 2003), http://www.campbellexpress.com/archives/070523/070523%2007%20Local.pdf [accessed January 30, 2008].

[32] Elizabeth Weintraub, "Buying Distressed Homes: Foreclosures, Short Sales, REOs," About, http://homebuying.about.com/od/4closureshortsales/qt/04074clshslreo.htm. [accessed January 15, 2008].

The Short Sale: A short sale is when a lender agrees to release the lien on a property for less money than the amount still on the mortgage. From 2002 through 2005, lenders funded $3 trillion in subprime loans. To date, the rate of foreclosures is running seven to twelve percent on many of these types of loans.

When the pay rate increases on these loans, that rate of foreclosure will soar. The average mortgage pay rate increase each year is forty-four percent. Couple that with an increased cost of living, including increased gas prices, and the average homeowner has a major problem.

Right now, there are millions of people who are behind on their mortgages. Unfortunately, many of these people are living in areas where home prices are falling and as the difference between what is owed on the home and what the home is worth becomes smaller, or even moves into the negative, we'll have a lot of people sitting on homes that are worth far less than what is owed. It's like being upside down on a car loan; in this situation, a short sale is the only answer, since there is no equity for a foreclosure.

REO: An REO (real-estate owned) is similar to buying a short sale, but in this case the property is already owned by the lender. This usually happens when no one bids enough at public auction to cover the amount owed.

These transactions are sometimes easier to complete because the occupants of the home are no long involved in the transaction.

Discounted Purchases

Fix and Flip: This is referred to as "putting lipstick on the pig." In these transactions, you do not do any large renovations, like those you see on television shows about property flipping. This is down and dirty—maybe just a little paint, new carpeting, landscaping or other minor repairs or upgrades. This is the purchase of a distressed property that you fix up and sell for a profit.

Time is the most important element in a fix and flip because the clock is always ticking, and time eats money. The average fix and flip is completed in one to three months, tops. Beyond three months, you could run into money problems and it could cost you dearly. After buying the property, the time goal is usually two weeks to complete repairs and turn the property back out to market.

Many investors use hard money to purchase these properties. Hard money comes in the form of a high-interest loan that only evaluates the loan-to-value in a deal and does not take into account your personal assets or credit score. Despite the high interest rates on hard money, it is worth it if you've run your numbers and you stick to your timeline for selling, because you can access it in a matter of days, which is crucial to acquiring a deal.

The key to the process is always knowing your after-repair value (ARV) and what your profit spread will be. The key to all real estate investing is knowing your math; remember, promoters and realtors lie, but math does not.

Wholesaling: This is purchasing a property at a deep discount and selling it to another investor who will either sell it to an owner/occupant or hold it for rental property. Simply put, it is finding a bargain property and passing it on to a bargain hunter.

According to real estate experts Charles and Kim Petty, "Your profit as a wholesaler should be between of $5,000 and $15,000 on each house. In some cases it will be higher than $15,000, and on some deals your profit may be a little lower than $5,000." [33]

According to the Pettys, there are a lot of reasons to go into wholesaling, but the most common include the quick cash, an excess of buying opportunities and the flexibility of the business.

Also, it's important to remember that when you decide to wholesale, your buyer should get a profit of instant equity. A lot of buyers of wholesaled properties want to turn them around quickly, so there has to be an almost instant profit built into the deal.[34] Wholesaling is one of the strategies that can become a full-fledged business, and you could quit your job to pursue it once you've become proficient at it.

---

[33] Charles and Kim Petty, "Wholesaling: Strategy for Real Estate Investors," Bigger Pockets, http://www.biggerpockets.com/articles/wholesaling-strategy-help.html [accessed December 2007].

[34] Petty, http://www.biggerpockets.com/articles/wholesaling-strategy-help.html.

Math is the most important side of any real estate acquisition and that is certainly the case in wholesaling. Doing the numbers and formulas is necessary in order not to get burned. You can use formal spreadsheets or simply learn to use your calculator, which will be indispensable.

Generally, wholesale opportunities are found through the following outlets:

1. Auction
    a. Government taxing authorities
    b. Banks
    c. Private
2. Hardship Sales
    a. Pre-foreclosure
    b. Divorce
    c. Probate of death
3. Contacts
    a. Realtors
    b. Birddogs (people who find deals)
    c. Real estate owned
4. Other
    a. Word of mouth
    b. Marketing
    c. Ads
    d. For sale by owner (FSBO)

In sum, if you have a desire to become a full-time real estate investor, wholesaling can create the opportunity. But, don't quit your day job without getting an excellent education and a few deals under your belt first. I want to make it perfectly clear that there is no replacement for proper education and mentorship when learning to act like an investor.

Lease Option: A lease option is an agreement between a seller and a buyer that allows the buyer to lease the property, with an option to buy it for an agreed-upon price during or after the lease is up. Sellers like lease agreements because the cash flow necessary to pay the mortgage and property taxes is provided by tenants who usually treat the property well because they might buy it.

No matter how slow the local real estate market might be, there is almost always a strong demand from lease option buyers. Many prospective homebuyers can afford the monthly payments, but they often have insufficient cash for a down payment, or have bad credit. The lease option solves this problem by giving the tenants/buyers a rent credit toward the down payment, as well as the opportunity to improve their credit scores. It's like a forced savings account. In addition, the tenants/buyers usually pay a nonrefundable consideration for the option upfront—typically, several thousand dollars.

Preconstruction: The preconstruction investing process is a real estate investment opportunity in which you buy tomorrow's homes at today's prices. Many real estate professionals refer to preconstruction sales as a "market within a market."

Bargain hunters have long been drawn to the preconstruction market because prices are lowest for those who commit the fastest. Preconstruction pricing typically advances rapidly after the opening is announced, which gives the average purchaser of a popular project very little time to reserve a unit at an early pricing stage. In many cases, prices change rapidly even before the project is announced and opened to the public, which makes it impossible for some buyers to participate at an ideal time.

In order to obtain the debt portion of their financing, developers must prove to the lending institutions that a demand exists for their projects. Sales offices, architectural renderings, floor plans and so on are created to pre-sell units at reduced proposed prices. During these phases, developers give incentives, such as various pricing levels that usually graduate upward as units are reserved.

From the reservation phase to the time of contract, or shortly thereafter, a total of ten to twenty percent of the purchase price is usually due. Timeframes and down payments differ from developer to developer. After the total down payment is made, there is usually no other payment required until the completion of construction, which is typically one to three years later.

If the buyer still has the unit at that point, he or she must close on the property through a mortgage or another payoff method. Some buyers keep properties for the long term and others decide to sell or flip them prior to completion of the construction, before the first mortgage payment is due. A buyer's purchase agreement will specify whether or not he or she can sell before closing. It is important for an investor to know all aspects of a development prior to purchasing a unit.

Done correctly, preconstruction investing has made millionaires out of ordinary people due to the low risk, low cost and minimal effort and skill required. Nonetheless, there is always an element of market risk and sometimes, preconstruction is akin to playing the stock market.

Conventional Investment Methods

Buy and Hold: With this strategy, investors learn how to use field-tested techniques to predict a property's market value, make smart buys and accumulate a steady increase in property value with time. You make your money when you buy the property; this technique requires proper market analysis and a study of the numbers on all your monthly outlay before you make a purchase.

Multi-family Dwellings: This involves purchasing residential structures with more than one dwelling unit. For example, there is multifamily housing, which is divided into two categories: two- to four-dwelling units (duplexes, triplexes and fourplexes) and units with five or more dwellings, commonly referred to as apartment buildings.

Multifamily housing may be tenant-occupied, owner-occupied (as in a condominium or cooperative project) or mixed, like many duplexes, with the owner occupying one side. I personally love this type of investment because multiple rents are better than one. If you have a duplex and one tenant moves out, at least you still have one rent covering some of your costs. This just gets better if you have a fourplex or venture into apartment units. Since most rental leases are for different periods, the possibility of having total vacancy is minimized.

Tax Benefits

When we discussed what an investment was in earlier chapters, we also decided that the better asset classes provide tax benefits, since taxes eat away at our overall returns. Not only is real estate a great investment, but it also offers numerous favorable tax benefits. Whether it is used as a residence or rental property, real estate offers taxpayers generous tax savings year after year.

Many people believe that real estate depreciation is the best tax deduction of all. Depreciation is a paper loss required for estimated wear, tear and obsolescence. Depreciating your properties helps offset some of the tax costs—and besides, the IRS requires real estate investors to depreciate their investment properties.

However, land value is not depreciable. This applies to 100 percent of the money invested in buying vacant land or land with a building on it. Condominiums do not have a land element and so 100 percent of the purchase price can be depreciated.

Residential income property is depreciated over twenty-seven and a half years on a straight-line basis. Commercial property is depreciated over thirty-nine years, also on a straight-line basis. When you couple ordinary depreciation with cost segregation, you increase your deductions. Cost segregation is used to depreciate personal property that is used in operating the property, such as appliances; these are depreciated over shorter periods, typically five to ten years. Even automobiles and trucks used in the investment operation can be depreciated over their useful lives.

If you are considered to be a "real estate professional" who meets a time requirement and materially participates in managing your investment property, you are allowed almost unlimited income tax deductions from your investment property. The law is constantly changing in this area, so this is not tax advice I'm giving here; property tax advice and proper preparation of your returns is essential, so seek a professional's counsel before jumping into such an investment. Find a CPA or other tax practitioner who is also a real estate investor, to ensure that he or she has a personal reason to be on top of the tax laws relating to real estate.

Time Requirement

If you spend at least 750 hours per year, or more than half of your working hours, involved in real estate activities, you probably qualify as a "real estate professional," though there does not appear to be any clear IRS ruling on a semi-retired person with no full-time occupation who devotes, say, 200 hours a year to real estate.

Full-time real estate brokers, realty sales agents, property managers, builders, contractors and leasing agents are examples of qualified real estate professionals. However, the tax law excludes real estate attorneys and mortgage brokers from qualifying, unless they spend more than fifty percent of their working hours investing in real estate. This would include managing, buying and selling real estate.

If you invest in real estate but do not qualify as a real estate professional, you are limited to an annual of maximum $25,000 in realty investment property loss deductions against your ordinary taxable income. This is called the "passive loss restriction" and includes the paper loss created by depreciation.

If your annual adjusted income exceeds $100,000, the $25,000 loss deduction gradually phases out. At the $150,000 adjusted-income level, the allowable tax loss deduction goes to zero. Any undeducted real estate investment tax loss is suspended for future use, for instance, when the property is sold at a profit. Then, you may subtract the unused, suspended tax loss from your capital gains to lower the taxable profit.

Material Participation

Participation in your real estate investment is critical. You can hire a professional property manager and still meet the material participation requirement, which allows you to claim the unlimited tax deductions as a professional. However, the IRS is really looking at this as a gap. Day-to-day operating details, such as collecting rents, evicting tenants and unclogging toilets can be delegated to the property manager, but *you* must make the major decisions, such as setting rents, approving major expenses and qualifying new tenants. This should all assist in meeting the time requirement.

The down side of depreciation is recapture. The maximum capital gains tax rate was reduced to fifteen percent in 2003 for assets owned for more than twelve months. (If held for less than twelve months, gains are taxed as ordinary income). However, the IRS requires that you "recapture" the tax savings from your income tax at a special twenty-five percent depreciation recapture tax rate when the property is sold. This applies whether or not you qualify as a real estate professional.

There is, of course, a strategy for getting around this and it involves a 1031 exchange, which is a tax code that allows for a "like kind" exchange of equal or more value. I suggest that you contact a competent tax advisor to determine when to use the 1031 exchange; an entire book could be written on its use.

Lastly, you can find a list of allowable rental expenses if you look at IRS Schedule E of Form 8825. Schedule E is used by individuals to report rental income and expenses, and Form 8825 is the same, just for partnerships, S corporations, estates and trusts. Some of the allowable expenses include:

1. Legal and other professional fees
2. Management fees
3. Mortgage interest (with exceptions)
4. Other loan interest
5. Repairs
6. Supplies
7. Taxes
8. Utilities

There are more; for a complete list, you can see the form. Just remember that there are also things you can't deduct, such as land and principal payments on mortgages.

As you can see, there are a lot of ways to offset rental income. But remember, the deductions have to be related to the rental property and can't be personal expenses. Don't get greedy; the IRS doesn't have a sense of humor.[35] Nonetheless, there are no tax benefits for your mutual fund, CD or other investment.

I want to make it clear, one last time, that this is not tax advice to rely on. This information is very general and may or may not apply to your situation. Prior to making any of the investments I've talked about here, you should seek out the best tax advisor you can. It's one of the best investments you can make, since taxes and expenses are two of the five destroyers of wealth; the others are procrastination, debt and inflation. You can read more about these in Chapter Eighteen.

Knowing When to Say "No"

Knowing what you plan to do with a property is critical, as is knowing what to do if an investment fails. This brings me to the idea of saying "no." A good investor understands that saying "no" is an important part of investing.

I've created a mnemonic to help investors check what to look for in an investment property:

EASTER™

1. Equity at purchase
2. Appreciation potential
3. Strong cash flow
4. Terrific location (retailers)
5. Easy management
6. Rent-ready

---

[35] Mark Minassian, "Tax Deductions for Landlords," About.com, http://biztaxlaw.about.com/od/dealingwithrealestate/a/landlordtaxes.htm?p=1 [accessed January 15, 2008].

I created the EASTER mnemonic because I see investors who haven't considered some of the basic questions when investing. The saddest thing I witness on a regular basis is novice investors walking in to my office after unwittingly buying ten or more properties, without a plan for what to do with them. I ask two threshold questions of these clients, to determine if they know what they're doing. If they look at me as if I've just spoken a foreign tongue, I know they are not properly educated investors.

The first question I ask is, "Did you buy these retail, wholesale or discount?" I have had a few blank stares on this one. The second thing I ask is, "What is your exit strategy on these properties?" This one has gotten some stares, too. This is a major problem.

The only way to avoid having a blank stare when asked these questions is to get educated and make your investing simple, by running the numbers and doing your due diligence. If you get the right education, you'll know the answers to both of these questions.

Timeshares Are Not Investments

I want to make it perfectly clear that a timeshare is not an investment, no matter what the telemarketer or salesperson at the presentation says. The Federal Trade Commission found that "only 3.3 percent of owners reported reselling their timeshares during the last 20 years. You may face competition from the original seller."[36]

Unfortunately, the money spent upfront on a timeshare does not go toward any real estate. Usually, three days after you've signed the contract, half of the money is paid out in commissions to the salesroom floor. The other half goes to telemarketers, gifts and other expenses related to getting you into the countless hours of high-pressure presentations that got you to buy in the first place. According the Federal Trade Commission, "Incomes generated by annual membership fees are more valuable than any title to real estate."[37]

---

[36] Wisconsin Department of Agriculture, Trade and Consumer Protection, "Timeshare Memberships and Resale Companies," http://datcp.state.wi.us/cp/consumerinfo/cp/factsheets/timeshares.jsp [accessed January 15, 2008].

[37] Wisconsin Department of Agriculture, Trade and Consumer Protection, "Timeshare Memberships and Resale Companies," http://datcp.state.wi.us/cp/consumerinfo/cp/factsheets/timeshares.jsp [accessed January 15, 2008].

Adding to the problem is that timeshare developers refuse to take back unwanted memberships because incomes generated by annual maintenance fees are more valuable than the members' titles to real estate. Timeshare owners say they have been unable to give away their memberships, much less find buyers.

Timeshare owners who discontinue use of the resort facilities must continue to pay their annual maintenance fees and any special assessments. If the members refuse to pay annual dues, the resort developer will sue or use a default judgment to recover back dues, interest and attorneys' fees. Members who have been down this road say that they felt trapped for life once they'd bought their timeshare. So, why get into this situation in the first place? Schedule nice vacations and when you're ready to invest, either call my office or go to your local real estate network to learn how not to get burned in a real estate deal.

The Media Says, "Don't Buy"

Let's take an historical look at how the media has tried to negatively influence the idea of buying real estate, and how real estate has continued to defy these prognosticators. In his book, *106 Mistakes Home Buyers Make...and How You Can Avoid Them*, Gary Eldred collected these priceless media quotes:[38]

- "The prices of houses seem to have reached a plateau, and there is reasonable expectancy that prices will decline."—*Time* magazine, 1947

- "Houses cost too much for the mass market. Today's average price is around $8,000—out of the reach for two-thirds of all buyers."—*Science Digest*, 1948

- "The goal of owning a home seems to be getting beyond the reach of more and more Americans. The typical new house today costs about $28,000." —*Business Week*, 1969

---

[37] Gary Eldred, 106 Mistakes Home Buyers Make...and How You Can Avoid Them (NY: Wiley and Sons, 1994), 71.

- "You might well be suspicious of 'common wisdom' that tells you, 'Don't wait, buy now...continuing inflation will force home prices and rents higher and higher.'"—*NEA Journal*, 1970

- "The median price of a home today is approaching $50,000... Housing experts predict price rises in the future won't be that great."—*Nations Business*, 1977

- "The era of easy profits in real estate may be drawing to a close."—*Money Magazine*, 1981

- "The golden age of risk-free run-ups in home prices is gone."—*Money Magazine*, 1985

- "Most economists agree... [a home] will become little more than a roof and a tax deduction, certainly not the lucrative investment it was through much of the 1980s." —*Money Magazine*, 1986

- "Financial planners agree that houses will continue to be a poor investment."—*Kiplinger's Personal Financial Magazine*, 1993

- "A home is where the bad investment is."—*San Francisco Examiner*, 1996

Despite all this forecasting, we just went through the period between 2000 and 2005, where appreciation levels were at historical highs and more millionaires were made overnight than in a year in Las Vegas.

In closing, I want you to understand that real estate agents are rarely educated on investing. In addition, the investment community does not have a way of being compensated on anything that is not securitized. Therefore, you'll have to educate yourself if you want to use real-estate investing as a way of creating wealth. Run your numbers and know what the entire deal means; think like an investor or businessperson. Remember that only one percent of people achieve real wealth, and out of them, seventy percent do it with real estate. That's a pretty good hint that real estate is a viable means to creating real wealth.

What We Learned

1. Get an excellent real estate investing education before you start.

2. You make your money before you purchase real estate—not when you sell.

3. Run your math; promoters and realtors lie, but math will keep the process honest.

4. Decide which real estate investing strategies work for you and go with them.

5. Tax benefits for real estate investing can be fantastic, so seek out a good tax preparer and advisor. Some like to prepare returns and not do any planning.

6. Start off with a financial blueprint by seeing an estate attorney. This will help avoid potential pitfalls that create setbacks.

7. Establish a set of policies and procedures for every key action your investment business must take, if you're going to be a full-time investor.

8. Create a team—e.g., a mortgage broker, a realtor, a lawyer, a contractor and whomever else you need to form a profitable investment business.

CHAPTER ELEVEN

Life Insurance: The Misunderstood Asset

What goes up but doesn't come down? The answer is properly structured, index-linked life insurance, because it uses all three pillars of wealth and protects you against negative changes in the market.

Life insurance is an asset that most people don't understand. It isn't as flashy as the funds you hear about, and most people consider it only as a protection for their loved ones in the event of the policyholder's death. But, properly structured life insurance can be a wonderful wealth-building tool—if it's used right.

Life insurance isn't the easiest of assets to understand when it's discussed in a cash flow creation role, so it's important that you seek out the advice of my office, or the office of another competent advisor who understands the ins and outs of life insurance. I will teach you what I can in this chapter, but your education should be ongoing.

One of the benefits of life insurance is that unlike investing in an equity fund or stocks, which negatively affect your account with a downturn in the market, index-linked life insurance protects your principal investment and provides an adequate return.[39]

Another benefit of life insurance is that cash value build-up acts like a tax-advantaged savings account, creating liquid cash flows. As you saw in Chapter Six, the performance history of 355 equity funds as a long-term strategy from 1970 to 2005 has been dismal. You need to reduce the fees and taxes you're paying in order to get

---

[39] Benjamin Graham, The Intelligent Investor (NY: Harper Business Essentials, 2003), 35.

ahead of the curve, and the proper use of the insurance chassis provides this.

A Brief History of Insurance

Insurance saw its beginnings as early as 5000 B.C. in China and 4500 B.C. in Babylon, where it was used as protection for traders. That was a form of commercial insurance. The concept of life insurance seems to have started in ancient Rome, where "burial clubs" paid for the funerals of their members and helped the surviving family members. This early from of insurance eventually led to modern life insurance, which started in late seventeenth century in England. The life insurance created there was also for the protection of traders, as it had been in ancient China, but this insurance was for the possible loss of life of the trader.[40]

Insurance first came to the United States in 1732, in Charleston, South Carolina, but that was limited to fire. In the late 1760s, the Presbyterian Synods in Philadelphia and New York founded the Corporation for Relief of Poor and Distressed Widows and Children of Presbyterian Ministers. This company would later become the New York Life Insurance Company. The late eighteenth and early nineteenth centuries saw dozens of life insurance companies started, though few survived.[41]

Life Insurance Products

This is not meant to be a comprehensive list of insurance products but a quick overview to educate you on the three major classifications of insurance products available to you. There is a great variety of life insurance products, and people who don't understand life insurance as an investment vehicle usually opt for the cheapest payment with the most coverage. People are not generally opposed to life insurance; they're only opposed to paying for it. I've polled people and asked them how much life insurance they would like if it were free and they uniformly say, "As much as I can get."

---

[40] Wikipedia contributors, "Life Insurance" Wikipedia, The Free Encyclopedia, http://en.wikipedia.org/wiki/Life_insurance#History [accessed Nov. 27, 2007].
[41] Wikipedia contributors, http://en.wikipedia.org/wiki/Life_insurance#History.

Term Life Insurance

Term life insurance is widely used because you can make the lowest premium payment possible to purchase the amount of death benefit you need to cover income and expenses. Term life insurance coverage is for a limited period of time, as the name indicates—usually five, ten, fifteen or twenty years. After that term, the insured can drop the policy or continue paying annually, increasing premiums to continue the coverage.

If the insured dies during the term, the death benefit will be paid to the beneficiary. Almost all owners of term life insurance fail to renew their policies at the end of the term because the rate is so high. In essence, if you don't die during the term, you've basically wasted your money.

Whole Life Insurance

The other category of insurance is permanent. This includes whole life insurance and universal life insurance. "Whole life" refers to a policy that pays a lump sum on death or, in some cases, the earlier diagnosis of a critical illness whenever it occurs, provided that the contract is kept in force and the required payments are made.

Universal Life Insurance

Universal life differs from whole life in that it is considered more flexible when it comes to premium payments. Often, whole life insurance will cost more, and the internal rate of return will not perform as well due to the mortality and administrative costs, thereby reducing your cash accumulation while you still live and breathe. In this chapter I'll show you some of the newer insurance products that create a tax-deferred cash flow, allow tax-free distributions[42] while you're alive (real life insurance), and protect you in the case of critical illness, which can wipe out even a well-planned fortune.

---

[42] Internal Revenue Code of the United States Code, Sections 72(e) and 7702 allow accumulations of cash values inside the insurance contract to accumulate tax-free under certain provisions of the contract.

Variable Universal Life Insurance

Variable universal life insurance (often shortened to VUL) is a type of permanent life insurance that builds cash value. In a VUL, the cash value can be invested in a wide variety of separate accounts, similar to mutual funds, and the choice of which of the available separate accounts to use is entirely up to the contract owner. The problem with this type of insurance contract is that it is fully tied to the market, and therefore is subject to the risk and volatility of the market. Many of these policies simply have not performed well because it is always difficult to time the market.

If we look at Benjamin Graham's definition of an investment and always look for protection of principal and adequate return, we can create the results we want over time. Variable universal life insurance as a product does not protect the principal, and while the return may be good sometimes, the final outcome is often disappointing.

Equity-indexed Universal Life Insurance

Equity-indexed universal life insurance (EIUL) works very similarly to traditional universal life insurance with the exception that the equity-indexed policy allows an individual to allocate excess premium payments to an account indirectly linked to the movements of a stock index. Essentially, the growth of the account mirrors an index, like the S&P 500.

Index investing has become popular with large funds and now, it's used with some universal life insurance policies as well. Indexed investing is fairly new for individual investors and it provides a conservative approach that many people like. Once the domain of institutional investors, index investing was opened to individual investors in 1976 through Vanguard. Because indexing seeks to match a market benchmark, the managers of these funds usually hold a sampling of the securities in an index. Because of this, indexing is sometimes called a passive approach because the managers don't get involved in as high a trade ratio as they might when trying to beat the market.[43]

---

[43] Ali Jaffery, "Understanding Indexing as an Investment Strategy," Contact Pakistan, http://www.contactpakistan.com/investment/investarticle07.htm [accessed December 2007].

The reason indexed investing has become so popular is the realization that most fund managers won't beat the market. We've learned, from John Bogle back in Chapter Six, that most funds underperform the market over time, so people figure that they should stop trying to beat the market and start trying to replicate its results. And now, there are crediting strategies to help you get involved through an EIUL product.

The index crediting method can be thought of as the process of calculating the index growth rate at the end of the index period. There are two primary index-crediting methods that are currently used: the annual point-to-point method and the daily averaging method.

Nearly every company offering equity-indexed universal life policies today offers the annual point-to-point method to calculate the index growth rate. With the annual point-to-point method, the beginning equity index value is recorded and compared to the ending equity index value at the end of the index period. If the ending index value is higher, interest is credited annually, subject to the participation rate and growth cap. If the ending index value is lower, no interest is credited. Essentially, if the market does well, then you do well. Over time, the market has done well, and the hope of the index-fund investor is that it continues to do so.

Annual Point-to-Point Index Crediting Method

The crediting of policies can get very intricate and confusing. I will try and illustrate it here, to give you a sense of how it might work in a given situation and what the outcome would be, but you absolutely need to sit down with a qualified planner to see how it would work in your particular circumstances.

The examples below illustrate two separate segment growth rates and how the index credits are calculated. We will assume that there is a 100-percent participation rate with a twelve-percent growth cap and a zero-percent growth floor using the annual point-to-point index crediting method. In other words, the most you can be credited is twelve percent and the lowest you will be credited for the index period will be zero percent, assuming you have a 100 percent participation rate.

Example one: The underlying index increases by nineteen percent from the beginning index segment date to the segment anniversary date.

The result will be based on the following formula: 100-percent participation rate multiplied by the nineteen-percent segment growth rate equals a nineteen-percent return subject to the twelve percent "growth cap," which equals a net twelve percent interest credit to the policy's cash value. In other words, if the underlying index goes past your growth cap, then you are credited with the maximum allowable interest.

Example two: The underlying index increases by seven percent from the beginning index segment date to the segment anniversary date.

The result will be based on this formula: 100-percent participation rate multiplied by seven-percent segment growth rate equals seven-percent return subject to the twelve-percent "growth cap," which equals a net seven-percent interest credit to the policy's cash value.

In addition to the growth floor, most EIUL policies offer a cumulative minimum guarantee, which provides for growth of cash values during a falling market and assures the policyholder that a minimum, guaranteed effective, annual interest rate is realized over a set period of time. For example, one company guarantees that over a five-year term, if the segment growth value doesn't reflect at least a two percent minimum effective annual interest rate, the segment value will be increased to that two percent level. This feature varies with each company, but most companies offer a version of this guaranteed minimum. The cumulative guarantee is another feature that makes equity indexed universal life insurance a unique and supreme cash accumulator that protects principal and provides an adequate return.

The Two Major Applications of Life Insurance

There are two main uses for life insurance from a goal-setting perspective. The first is succession capital, which is what people generally hear about in regards to how it will protect their families or estate in case the breadwinner departs. It's the money your family or estate receives in the case of your death.

However, you also have lifestyle capital, which is designed to create future tax-free cash flows as supplemental retirement income. Unlike your pension plan, which will be taxed as ordinary income in your tax bracket, this income can be distributed tax-free.

If you are not thinking about your net "spendable" income (NSI) in your retirement years, then you're not developing a winning wealth plan. You need to know exactly how much you'll need to maintain your lifestyle when you retire. You'll also need to factor in the costs of increasing medical needs.

Succession Capital

Using other people's money, or leverage, to increase your own financial gain is an established practice. Today, though, leverage is being used to purchase life insurance, and has gotten the attention of insurance promoters and financial professionals. But, does the concept hold water, or is it just another way for people to sell life insurance?[44] I'm going to explain the concept as much as I can, to show you how it is possible to make this arrangement work. It's important, though, to examine all the angles before trying something like this.

How Premium Financing Works

Premium financing means borrowing money to pay the premiums on the life insurance so that available capital is spared. This method can also lower out-of-pocket costs and potential gift taxes.

The lender bases the current loan interest rate on the one-year London Interbank Offering Rate (LIBOR), adding a profit margin spread of 175 to 250 basis points. Essentially, lending rates are determined on a case-by-case basis, taking into consideration the loan

---

44 Andre Blaze, "Life Insurance Premium Financing—What to Look For," Capital Maximization Strategy, January 24, 2005, http://www.capmaxstrategy.com/non-frames/AICPA%20-%20Article%20-%20What%20to%20Look%20For.pdf.

amount and the lenders' risk exposure. Loan interest rates can be fixed on an annual basis, but may vary from year to year, based on fluctuations in LIBOR or changes in the borrower's financial conditions, which must be updated annually.

You must ask yourself some questions before investing in this type of vehicle because if there are additional fees, such as loan origination fees (commonly 0.5 to 1.25 percent of the expected total loan balance), associated with the loan, they can offset any savings related to a low interest rate. Often, these fees must be paid upfront, but some lenders allow them to be financed with the policy premiums.

In addition, is the interest variable or fixed? If variable, how often does it reset? In most arrangements, the interest is a variable rate, with a portion of the interest determined by an index resetting each year, but the spread on top of the index may be fixed for the life of the loan.

The twelve-month LIBOR is a common index as well as the prime rate. If there is a fixed interest rate, it is important to determine how long it will be fixed. In many instances, the fixed rate is only fixed for a certain time period, such as five or ten years. A cap will be set on how high the loan interest rate can go during the loan term. So, while the loan interest might be variable, there is a cap that will limit how high the interest rate can grow, such as eight percent.

You can also secure what's called a "collar," which is when a loan has both a cap and a floor on the interest rate. It basically keeps the interest rate from spiraling too high but ensures that the lender can charge a minimum in exchange for that security.[45]

Caps are more expensive than collars because caps protect only the consumer, while collars offer some protection to the lender. Because of this, the extra costs are usually built into a loan origination fee or into the amount of spread placed in the offer. Caps and collars are usually only offered on loans greater than $1 million.[46]

---

[45] John A. Oliver, "Premium Financing as Tool for Life Insurance Funding," American Bar Association,
http://www.abanet.org/rppt/meetings_cle/2005/spring/pt/ExcitingWealthPlanning/OLIVER_HARRISON_hand.pdf [accessed December 2007].
[46] Blaze, http://www.capmaxstrategy.com/non-frames/AICPA%20-%20Article%20-%20What%20to%20Look%20For.pdf.

The best candidates for premium-financed life insurance typically have a minimum net worth of $5 million. Collateral for the loan usually consists of personal assets and can be reduced by the cash value in the policy being financed.

The power of premium financing lies within the same simple concepts related to the leveraging of permanent life insurance for estate liquidity and wealth-transfer planning. The key is to evaluate premium financing not as a standalone transaction, but as an alternative to the traditional funding of life insurance using the same capital base.

According to Scott McVicker, formerly of National Underwriter Life and Health, the single greatest misconception that some planners have is that the client must have an arbitrage opportunity for the financed transaction to provide a benefit over traditional funding. The power of premium financing is based on the leveraging effect it creates by combining the financing piece of the equation with a properly designed life insurance policy, so that one of the secret pillars predominates over the other.[47]

I have been involved in cases where it made sense not to drain cash flow and instead use leverage to accomplish payments of the life premiums. If the structure is designed properly, it can have an exit strategy built in. There is also one planning technique for families that have done no estate planning but are uninsurable and have healthy children. This planning tool is too technical to discuss here, but if you're reading this and know someone who has an illness, no estate plan and over $10,000,000 of net worth, you can have them give my office a call.

Lifestyle Capital

Many investors are unaware that cash-value life insurance is the only investment tool that acts as a self-completing college fund and a supplemental retirement savings plan, and can be creditor-proof in some states. A great argument these days is that the cash value build-

---

[47] Scott McVicker, "Premium Financing: It's The Retained Capital, Stupid!" National Underwriter, Vol. 108, No. 41, Nov. 1, 2004.

up is the functional equivalent of a retirement plan garnering comparable protection. Fabulous features include the ability to build up and not count this cash value as an asset for the purpose of financial aid when your children head off to college. Finally, by overfunding a cash-value life insurance policy up to the modified endowment contract (MEC)[48] guidelines, it can become investment-grade life insurance.

Before things get a little technical, let's discuss some important points. You can save with a life insurance policy and earn as high as 8.5 percent interest tax-free. I know of a carrier that has a product that can consistently earn this rate of return. You keep the death benefit as low as you can within the guidelines of the tax code, since the investment isn't really geared toward the death benefit; you want dollars to live on.

After a few years of saving tax-free, you can take the money back out, tax-free, to the extent you need it to supplement your retirement income. This is far better than traditional retirement plans, since those are taxed at ordinary tax rates, and tax rates are going up.

"Overfunding" an Equity Indexed Life Policy

"Overfunding" is a strategy that focuses on accumulating cash in a life insurance policy rather than on the death benefit, which is the payout to your loved ones when you pass away. This approach leverages the highest policy premium allowed (the most you are allowed to contribute) against the lowest life insurance death benefit allowed so that your cash accumulation exceeds your policy net insurance costs. This technique usually takes about ten years to become really effective, but when it does it offers tremendous potential for tax-deferred cash accumulation.

There are four fundamental steps to determining the combination of maximum premiums and minimum death benefits necessary to selecting the most leveraged indexed universal life policy:

---

[48] A modified endowment contract is defined as any life insurance contract entered into on or after June 21, 1988, that meets the life insurance requirements of Code §7702, but which fails to meet a special seven-pay test or is received in exchange for a modified endowment contract, Internal Revenue Code of the United States Code, section §7702A(a).

First, make sure that you can actually keep to the payment commitments before jumping into this method. In order to really make this method effective, you need to stick to a schedule.

Also, you need to find out what the minimum "face amount" is under the Deficit Reduction Act of 1984. The face amount is the value of the payout from the insurance in the event of death, and there are minimum requirements legislated by the government concerning this type of insurance.

Next, you need to examine closely the internal rate of return of any potential investment policy. A lot of agents will promise eight percent or more, but I find that rate unrealistic. I usually calculate a rate of 5.25 percent for my clients, which still beats most investments because it's tax-deferred.

Once you've determined your premium commitment and face value, you have to find out what the maximum allowable premiums are under the tax code.[49] Essentially, this part of the tax code provides a test for determining how large the premiums could be during a seven-year period while still allowing for tax-free cash surrender withdrawals from the indexed fund.

Once you've settled all of these things, the maximum premium is set is and the policy can be built with an eye toward the overfunding strategy. You've got to remember, though, that this strategy will not work for everyone. Certain requirements and minimums should be met, and you'd be wise to find a very well-informed advisor before committing to something like this. This is a long-term strategy and it's going to take time for the build-up to take effect.[50]

Legislation That Can Affect Overfunding

There are several pieces of legislation that affect the concept of overfunding. These include the previously mentioned TAMRA and the Deficit Reduction Act (DEFRA) of 1984. These rules can get very complex, but they directly affect the allowable limits in

---

[49] IRS Code 7702A of the Technical and Miscellaneous Revenue Act (TAMRA) of 1998.
[50] "Strategies for Buying Equity Indexed Universal Life Insurance," MEG Financial, http://www.equityindexeduniversallifeinsurance.com/eiul_strategies.htm (accessed December 2007). This is a great compilation of the strategy and tax laws related to the use of insurance as an investment.

funding a life insurance policy, the minimum death benefit based on the age of the insured, and the amount of the premiums paid, so it's important that you know they're out there. A good tax attorney and a good financial advisor who is familiar with overfunding of an equity-indexed life insurance policy should be able to help you at least garner a basic understanding of the legislation and how it affects you. If you're not careful, your policy could end up being flagged if it fails to meet regulations set up by the Internal Revenue Code.[51]

Accessing the Savings

The reason you're able to access your savings in the cash value tax-free is because it will be characterized as a loan. This is a so-called "wash loan" because the interest rate the borrower pays and the interest rate the insurer pays on the cash value are the same, so each rate "washes out" or equalizes the other.

For example, suppose that the current rate the insurer is paying on the cash value account is seven percent, and that the policy loan rate is six percent. With a wash loan, the seven-percent rate would be reduced to six percent, to match the loan rate. Fixed, indexed and wash are the three loan options offered by many carriers these days. The goal is to use leverage to create more wealth with the right insurance framework, and if it has a dynamic loan provision, you can make money on dollars that you've taken out by taking advantage of arbitrage, which builds your cash flows. This can happen with certain insurance products that credit 140 percent of the S&P on borrowed cash values in the policy.

To illustrate, the loan interest rate is five percent; you get credited 140 percent of the S&P (up to a cap of ten percent), which in this case creates seven percent minus the five percent loan rate, and you are left with a net result of two percent on money that is no longer in the policy. To understand this better, you should talk to a qualified professional planner.

---

[51] The Deficit Reduction Act of 1984 (DEFRA) and the Technical and Miscellaneous Revenue Act of 1988 (TAMRA).

Some Final Thoughts on the Tax Implications of Using Life Insurance to Build Cash Value

As with any asset and financial blueprint, you have to be careful of the tax implications, since taxes are the biggest expense you'll pay in your lifetime. If you want to have free control of the cash values in your policy, then you'll have to run the risk of passing away before you get a chance to spend it.

While the transfer of the death benefit transfers to your beneficiary free of income tax, the proceeds are included in your estate for the purposes of estate tax. That's why many times, an irrevocable life insurance trust (ILIT) or life insurance partnership (LIP) is created. The policies are either purchased by the entity or transferred to the entity if the policy preexists. When transferred, it is considered a gift and requires some particularized planning in order not to exhaust a lifetime gift-tax credit.

In my opinion, there are too few planners out there having the estate and gift tax discussion with their clients. In addition, they are not having a discussion about whether transferring to a tax-beneficial entity makes sense for a client who does not need regular annual payments from the cash values of the policy. I find this to be a little thoughtless, and we may see a number of fallouts from this incomplete planning as people begin to pass away.

When I've asked advisors about this, they've always stated that they only work with middle-class folks who won't have to worry about estate tax. They must be clairvoyant, able to see what legislation is coming down the pike.

Perhaps the biggest downside to using investment-grade life insurance, if you can consider it a downside, is that the best results are reserved for those who are young and healthy. If you are not healthy, your internal insurance costs are going to be higher, which reduces the internal rate of return and significantly affects your outcome. In addition, some people may be severely ill or at an age where it will be impossible to have this strategy make sense.

I am seeing some planners use this strategy for everyone, which I disagree with. I think the best results will come to those who have more time and are in excellent health. While you can overlook some of the health at a standard rating on the policy, you would want to make sure you have ten or more years to take advantage of the time value of money. The alternative to having time is funding with a large dump and then making higher monthly payments—or, preferably, annual payments at the beginning of each year—to get the quickest benefit of time and interest.

Lastly, as we have examined, and as I alluded to earlier in this chapter, the use of the equity indexed universal life insurance meets the Graham definition of an investment because it protects your principal, your return is almost guaranteed, and with the crediting methods and the minimum fixed guarantee, you will always get an adequate return. When you couple the safety of this investment method with the ability to use it as a loan to yourself at any time, you have the elusive liquidity that most other forms of investment don't offer.

What We Learned

1. Consider proper life insurance for your tax-free supplemental retirement income. The ideal situation is for a couple to get two policies that they can use in retirement, rotating their usage. For example: Harry and Jane purchase two policies. They use Harry's cash-surrender value to live on for five years and then switch to Jane's policy and use loans on her policy for five years, as Harry's goes up again. The couple can alternate the use of each policy every five years or so.

2. Indexing is a "passive" investment approach emphasizing broad diversification and low portfolio trading activity.

3. Over time, the broad stock market indexes have outperformed the average general equity fund.

4. If you have a larger estate and like the idea of leverage, you'll want to consider premium finance so that you don't reduce available cash flow.

5. Find a carrier that credits your loan at 140 percent of the S&P so that even when you're taking your money out, you're making money for a win-win.

6. You can use leverage to create more wealth with the right insurance product than you would with traditional equity funds; if it has a dynamic loan provision, you can make money on dollars that you take out, using an arbitrage that creates your cash flows.

CHAPTER TWELVE

Five Steps Inside the Pillars of Wealth

Contained within the Three Secret Pillars of Wealth are five steps that I advocate taking when the time is right, and when you're in an investor's mindset. The five steps are of a cyclical nature and can be repeated as often as necessary in order to accomplish your personal wealth accumulation or retirement goals.

It's important to understand that using the three pillars of wealth will take commitment, knowledge and regulation. But, if used properly, there's no limit to how much wealth you can create. And even if you're not looking to become a self-made billionaire like the ones we've mentioned in previous chapters, you should be thinking about how much cash flow you'll need to retire comfortably. By following the five steps inside the three pillars, you can prepare a secure future for yourself and your family.

Step 1: Education

The first and maybe most important step you'll take on your journey to retirement freedom is educating yourself. Before taking any action using the Three Secret Pillars of Wealth, you need to understand exactly what they are, and how they'll benefit you in your quest for wealth.

Take advantage of the technologies available today. Use webinars and podcasts from reputable financial advisors who I recommend—ones who know the principles behind the three pillars and can help you understand the subject matter. Learn how to calculate the costs and returns of potential investments and make sure you're considering all of the possible pitfalls when you crunch those numbers. We are doing several webinars monthly because it is cost-effective and nonthreatening to the listener. We also have live seminars forming across the country as we train strategic partners who can offer authentic assistance to motivated, freethinking investors.

One of the most important aspects of the educational phase will be learning when to disregard "conventional" wisdom. Remember that just because most people think something is right doesn't make it so. As we saw in some earlier chapters, many people think that paying off their mortgages early is a sure way to achieve retirement nirvana. Well, we've proven that that isn't always the case. The numbers just don't add up when you consider how much wealth could have been created by these people if they paid themselves first rather than early payment of their mortgages. Don't assume anything. Think about what you've invested in and make a decision based on the numbers, not convention.

Step 2: Harvest

The next step will be to harvest the dollars you currently have trapped in underperforming investments. This will take a serious evaluation of where your money is currently held, and whether those venues are the best ways for you to create wealth.

As we talked about in previous chapters, home equity is a powerful tool that should be used while your home is still standing. With the intrinsic leverage in your home's equity, you can capture arbitrage opportunities by parlaying a simple interest home equity loan into greater gains through tax-advantaged investment vehicles that offer compound interest, such as an equity-indexed universal life insurance policy.

The same can be said for the equity in your business. Using that equity to create wealth will aid in forming an exit strategy. It makes sense to use the equity in your business while you're still the owner, and while it's still viable. You never know how long your business will be profitable and how long you'll want to stay on board.

By examining your current investments, you'll likely find that some of them are keeping your money captive, and that by freeing your money, you'll create a clearer path to retirement security. We've discussed how mutual funds and inadequate pensions are going to be a major concern over the next several years, and how keeping your money in these underperforming, insecure vehicles is asking for trouble. You want to put your money into something that's going to give you control and a sheltered return on investment. Pensions are often composed of small IRAs that limit contributions to $4,000 a year, or 401(k)s where contributions aren't matched by your employer. You can do better with your money.

Step 3: Deploy

Once you understand the workings behind the three pillars and have analyzed the state of your money, you're ready to start deploying your money into quality investment vehicles that will provide a return on your investment with some protection from taxes and other expenses, such as management fees. In addition, you'll be looking for the pillar of arbitrage in order to capture a profit in a situation that returns more than it costs you.

Cash Value Equity Indexed Universal Life Insurance

As we discussed in the last chapter, there is probably no better investment than indexed life insurance, if it's properly structured. While there are many products out there, most of them are not well structured by the carriers, and the agents who sell these products usually don't understand them at all. If you find an advisor who does and he can articulate the internal rate of return over the insurance costs, you have a real champion. If he knows the best crediting strategies to go with these products, he is above average.

The two things that devastate your returns are expenses and taxes. You know that by using the life insurance chassis, you'll eliminate most if not all of the tax hit on your investment. The right product will also eliminate most of the expenses seen in lesser products, and you'll be head and shoulders above the crowd, which relies on mutual funds or other volatile investments that carry expenses from greedy managers. Most funds have a level expense ratio, which means that as your pot grows, so do the expenses, rather than shrinking over time with your growth, like a proper insurance policy would.

To review, the ideal place for retirement dollars will have four characteristics:

1. It should have downside protection
2. It should have tax efficiency
3. It should reduce expenses
4. It should provide an adequate return in a less-robust market

The only way to get all four of these desirable components is by using properly structured life insurance. If you're opposed to life insurance or have significant health issues, that's no problem. You can think about using real estate as the focus of your investing, but you need leverage in real estate and often, that means debt leveraging (loans). As a precaution, it makes sense to have a death benefit to cover that debt, so you would still want life insurance.

Tax-free Bonds

Municipal bonds are bonds issued by state and local government agencies. The federal government exempts the interest income on these bonds from federal income taxes, the idea being that since the money from the bond issue is going to fund infrastructure or needed government services, the federal government will lend support to these governmental bodies by not taxing the interest. Also, it makes this vehicle more attractive to investors.

The tax-free status allows the issuing government agency to borrow money at a lower interest rate. Investors buy these tax-free issues because on a tax-equivalent basis, the returns are at or above the interest rates they would earn on a comparable-risk taxable bond.

The downside to investing in tax-free municipal bonds is you have to buy them from a broker, or as shares in a mutual fund. By owning them directly, you are guaranteed the return of your principal, as long as you own them long enough; but, generally, you have to own a minimum value of $5,000 in bonds and at least $25,000 in investments to make a good gain on them.

This use of the brokerage increases fees, but if you run the numbers, it might not be as bad as all the fees associated with other funds. And, because they are tax-free in build-up, you've eliminated that expense. Probably the biggest drawback is that any use of the return is going to be taxed; therefore, you do not get a tax-free income like you would with the life insurance chassis.

Additional Real Estate: Purchasing a Second Property Using Leverage

Purchasing an "investment property," as they're called these days, was in vogue during the housing boom that lasted until early 2006. People were purchasing homes at outrageous prices on the promise that one day soon, they could sell the homes for tremendous profits. The problem was, many of those same people failed to follow the first step in our five-step process for deploying the three secret pillars of wealth: education. By researching the real estate market and having an exit strategy, many people could have protected themselves from paying too much, or ending up in foreclosure. Work the numbers; understand whether or not you have the money to make an investment like this.

Purchasing a second home or rental property can be a significant addition to your portfolio, and there are opportunities to use leverage to purchase several properties on a short timeline. Using the equity you have in one property, you can purchase a second, and so on, until you have yourself a nicely padded real estate portfolio. But don't be fooled. That kind of move should be made with the advice and counsel of a professional who has experience in purchasing real estate as an investment.

Real estate purchasing is one of the best opportunities to use leverage. Because there are so many mortgage options, leverage is more readily customizable in real estate than in many other investment vehicles. The beauty of real estate is that you can get someone else to pay your debt service by renting out your investment properties. Real estate can also help generate cash flow, which is the third pillar of wealth we discussed. Cash flow from your real estate investments can then be used for long-term retirement investing.

Real estate also adds the benefit of appreciating in value while generating cash flow—a double whammy, if you will.

Step 4: Secure

Whenever we accumulate assets, we want to make sure we are doing so efficiently, and that means doing it in accord with our financial blueprint. Builders uses blueprints to build homes, and builders of wealth must use blueprints to give themselves direction, purpose and clarity, and to avoid unnecessary fees like probate or estate taxes.

Basic Estate Planning and Asset Protection

Estate planning and asset protection are good ideas for everyone, regardless of their net worth, marital status, age or gender. Estate planning allows you to plan for incapacity and death, thus avoiding the need for a conservatorship or probate, both of which are time-consuming, intrusive and expensive.

The basic plan incorporates a living trust, pour-over will and general assignment for the departure documents, and then provides for incapacity with a durable power of attorney and healthcare directive. There are over 160 strategies one could add to the base plan to accomplish charitable and death tax reduction for champion investors who accumulate extraordinary wealth.

Securing assets also means acting responsibly for your family in the event that you depart prematurely or require long-term care. If you own multiple properties around the country and they all have mortgages on them, I don't think it is responsible or intelligent to be without adequate life insurance to cover the mortgages, should you pass away. In the same vein, I think it is equally irresponsible not to have protection in place for disability or nursing home care, since no one has a crystal ball and the likelihood of either of these things happening is seven in ten.

There will be more on financial blueprinting and estate planning in Chapter Seventeen.

Step 5: Review

After each cycle of the five steps, you need to review and collect your financial equilibrium. This means that you must reassess the deployment and make sure the numbers still work; otherwise, you might have to make adjustments.

In the military, they cannot afford to waste opportunities that save lives, so they have to make quick decisions. Sometimes, in the heat of a quick decision, when you get to the reassessment phase, you'll find that you need to improvise, adapt and overcome some of the consequences of your decisions. I've noticed a condition that I refer to as "ostriching," wherein clients bury their heads in the sand and refuse to take action and responsibility for the situations they've created. If make-believe were this easy, all we would have to do is close our eyes and wish we were wealthy and it would happen, but unfortunately, that is not the case.

I make clients confront and deal with their finances and sometimes, it is not pretty. I had to do this in my own life, after having a string of bad partnerships and business relationships that left me wallowing. All you can do is pick yourself up out of the trench and move forward with a true instinct for survival and clarity of purpose. Until you have this clarity when it comes to accumulating wealth and becoming an educated investor, you'll be at the mercy of a system that does not favor you and is often in the hands of people who don't know what they're doing.

The reassessment of your investment plan needs to happen periodically, whether you've just cycled through the steps or not, because things change and sometimes, they do so at light speed. Depending on the complexities of a person's holdings, review may be required every quarter, semi-annually or annually. I have even seen situations wherein clients have acted like business octopi, with a new business tentacle extending out every month. People like this need guidance monthly, lest they shoot themselves in the feet.

There are no hard-and-fast rules dictating when it's the right time to cycle through the five steps again. It is sometimes an individual choice and may even be a gut-check with some folks. Remember: without guts, there's no glory. Now, having said that, I don't mean that you should put it all on the line, but you can take calculated risks, and there is often enough time to make adjustments as you go.

If you own a number of real properties, there may be frequent windows of opportunity to cycle by harvesting and deploying. Not only is it a good asset-protection strategy to remove the equity when possible, but it makes perfect sense to place it where it can begin to earn interest and is liquid. Again, I know people whose paid-off homes in Laguna Beach, California, have slid down mountainsides. If they could take time back and take out equity loans for the purpose of investment, do you think they wouldn't?

Taking the right action means doing what feels right according to your own heart and intuition, not anyone else's standards. To distinguish the right action from a "should," use the following rule of thumb: A "should" may feel uninteresting. The right action, according to your heart, always feels freeing and energizing, and eventually becomes a "must."

If you take no action at all, it is because it falsely appears to be safe, but think about the deer in the headlights that freezes up and takes no action: It usually ends up strapped to the car's hood. Similarly, if you take no action to provide yourself and think that the government and your employer will take care of you for the thirty to forty years you might be retired, think again.

Ask yourself, "What would I dare to be wealthy?" If you're not interested in being wealthy, that is fine. But what would you dare in order to be provided for until your passing day? The years ahead are going to be scary in terms of higher costs for everything—including gas at $5 per gallon and homes and education at incredible prices, not to mention food. If your only plan for retirement is something that is going to be taxed in the higher brackets, I hope you make it. If, on the other hand, you're committed to a life of freedom that is not full of fear of the future, then I applaud you. This is bold and brave, and just what this country was designed for.

What We Learned

1. Educate yourself on the Three Pillars of Wealth and create a plan of action wherein they are available in relation to your situation.

2. Consider harvesting trapped dollars if you don't currently have savings or discretionary income.

3. Deploy the trapped and underutilized dollars into vehicles that create tax advantages or tax-free opportunities, and reduce expenses over time, since those are two killers of wealth.

4. Secure your accumulations with proper estate planning and asset protection.

5. Review and redo when applicable.

CHAPTER THIRTEEN

Retirement Planning

We know, because of our aging population, that providing Social Security to future retirees will require higher taxes or reduced benefits. And, as we've discussed throughout this book, the traditional retirement formula is going to leave you broke. The wide use of mutual funds, tied to market volatility, that contain both disclosed and concealed fees is just not reliable. If you consider John Bogle's insightful examination of 355 funds over a thirty-five-year period, there is no question that most mutual funds are not where you want your retirement dollars. Even if you find a good index fund, it may be so overly saturated that getting ahead will require some form of miracle.

Retiring securely is going to take action, and a good understanding of what your options are. Most people leave their retirement planning to their place of employment and simply roll their 401(k) into a different one when they change jobs. But do you really understand what a 401(k) does, and how much in taxes you'll owe when you retrieve the money? Do you even know when you're eligible to take the money in the first place? In this chapter, I'll try to help you understand your options and tell you what I think is the best course of action.

Don't Leave Your Planning to Someone Else

Corporate pension plans can't be trusted like they could be when your mother and father were starting out. Against a backdrop of spiraling medical costs, failing pension plans and the uncertain future of Social Security, American workers will need to resort to new, creative measures beyond just their companies' 401(k) plans.

Warning signs are plentiful that more individuals could reach retirement age without as much money as they need. During the past six years alone, companies have killed off more than 640 underfunded corporate retirement plans, affecting the retirement of some three quarters of a million people.

In 2006, International Business Machines Corp. (IBM) said that it would freeze its US pension plans in 2008, affecting 117,000 employees, instead of improving its workers' 401(k) plan. General Motors Corp. also announced in 2006 that they'd stopped making matching contributions to the 401(k)s of its executive employees. If you are not getting a dollar-for-dollar match, putting money into a pension plan is practically a losing proposition.

The Employee Retirement Income Security Act of 1974 (ERISA) mandates that companies create a separate entity dedicated to funding pension benefits for current and future retirees. ERISA and the Financial Accounting Standards Board (FASB) dictate how these pension trusts are to be set up and funded.

Unfortunately, in recent years, many of these trusts have been underfunded. According to Howard Silverblatt of *Businessweek*, "At the close of 2004, S&P 500's defined-benefit plans as a group had $1,265 billion in assets and $1,430 billion in liabilities. That $164.3 billion in underfunding barely changed from the $164.8 billion underfunded position a year earlier in 2003, and in 2005 underfunding increased to nearly $182 billion."[52]

Silverblatt's findings are a frightening reminder that many pensions are tied to the volatility in the market and that depending on underfunded, volatile pension trusts is a mistake.

On top of those negatives, there are numerous errors and problems found in pensions and profit sharing programs that can rob you of your ability to get ahead, and they start with a lack of control. In other words, just because you have your check debited each month,

---

[52] Howard Silverblatt, "America's Other Pension Problem," Businessweek.com Dec. 19, 2005. http://www.businessweek.com/investor/content/dec2005/pi20051219_9796_pi015.htm [December 19, 2005].

don't think that things are on autopilot. Read your statements and ask questions, because your pension plan is run by people, and people make mistakes.

It's not unusual for companies to change plans, sell themselves to another company, merge with another company, change their compensation packages and more. The National Center for Retirement Benefits, Inc. has identified thirty common errors made in the administration of pension and profit sharing plans. They are as follows:

1. Your employer's plan calls for all compensation paid to you to be used in determining your retirement benefits. Your bonuses and overtime were deleted from the computer run, resulting in a portion of the contributions and benefits that should have been accumulated for you being unpaid.

2. The administrators credited your profit sharing account with the forfeitures and earnings from the wrong year.

3. You are leaving a profit sharing plan and the administrators have valued your account on the basis of the fair market value of the assets at the beginning of the year, instead of at the end of the year when the stock market had increased substantially.

4. The administrators have cashed you out of the plan on the basis of an old vesting schedule rather than the new, more favorable schedule.

5. For purposes of vesting, the administrators failed to include your service with a related company.

6. You're in the profit sharing plan but the administrators have failed to include you in the pension plan, even though you qualify.

7. You're being cashed out of your employer's pension plan and the administrators have used the wrong years of service for you in determining your benefits.

8. The wrong computer disk is being used to update files. Your current benefit statement reflects the same information that was on your benefit statement four years ago!

9. Many years after you leave a company and reach age sixty-five, there is no pension distribution paid to you, as the company you worked for is out of business or has moved to a new location and has changed its name, and you don't know how to find it.

10. The company has numerous divisions and each one has a different plan. The administrator is working on cashing you out of the pension plan but is using the information from another division's plan.

11. Your service with one division was not counted toward the pension plan of another division. As you leave your employer, it is preparing to pay you substantially less than you're entitled to receive.

12. The plan trustees have improperly invested your plan money and, as a result, you are getting a payout that is a fraction of what you should receive.

13. The staff from the plan administration department is constantly turning over and no one is familiar with your file.

14. After many years of continuous service, the plan administrators show you having a break in service of several years when, in fact, you had no such break in service.

15. Your company merged with another and the benefits of the new plan do not give you the minimum benefit promised by the old plan. Furthermore, the executives and plan administrators from the old company are no longer available to help you.

16. Computer software used by the plan administrators has serious design flaws.

17. You went from union to non-union status. The administrators failed to take into consideration your union benefits when determining your total benefits.

18. Your pension plan was amended to raise benefits but the administrators are still using the old benefit formula.

19. The company counts your five highest compensation years of service toward retirement. When calculating your benefits they used your last five years and failed to review your compensation from many years ago, when commissions you earned resulted in much higher compensation that should have been used in calculating your benefits.

20. Your employer entered into prohibited transactions that resulted in the loss of substantial funds for the participants in its plans. A prohibited transaction is an investment the law does not allow.

21. Your supervisor incorrectly reported your wages to the benefits department.

22. Your plant is closing down or you are part of a large group of employees that are being discharged. There are Internal Revenue Service rules that could make you 100 percent

vested even though your employer has treated you as only partially vested.

23. As a participant in your employer's plan you are making contributions from your own money in addition to what your employer contributes. When you leave the company the administrators fail to include the benefits funded by your own money.

24. Many years ago you participated in a plan that was discontinued by your employer. The administrator "froze" the plan (meaning no more contributions would be made to that plan, but as people left the company, the plan would pay them their rightful share). Now, many years later, you are leaving the company and the administrators pay you from the current plans but not the "frozen" plan.

25. The administrators fell behind in their work and contributions and benefits were not posted to your account. Furthermore, one or more years later, no one caught this error.

26. Your employer illegally took money from the pension or profit sharing trust. Now, as you retire, there is insufficient money available to fund your retirement.

27. Records were destroyed or misplaced and the employees were not told about it. As the administrative staff does its work, they are trying to reconstruct your files for many, many years.

28. You're eligible for early retirement but no one has informed you. Had you been told, you would have been able to take your money out in a lump-sum distribution.

29. The pension fund administrators are working with a plan that provides for various benefit options and requires many complex calculations to determine the highest benefits for you. They make a mistake and pay you on the basis of the option with the least amount of money.

30. Wrong assumptions and methods were used to determine your benefits. Had the correct tables been used you would have received substantially more money.[53]

It is possible for any one or a combination of these errors to occur in your company offered plan, and I don't think you want to have it as your one and only strategy for retirement.

It's clear that workers are going to have to save more, stay on the job longer and pay more attention to the investment vehicles that are used to fund their pensions if they want comfortable retirements. The dream that you could get out of your office at fifty-five (still young enough to enjoy life) and start setting up perpetual tee times is over. You won't be able to afford it, and your employer can't afford it, either.

To help you better understand what plans are on offer and what benefits and pitfalls they have, I'll explore some of the more common ones here.

Traditional Plans

Defined contribution plans or employer plan with a match. In my mind, this is the only employer plan you'll want to look at, and only if it is a dollar-for-dollar match. If your employer matches your contributions to the company's defined contribution plan, e.g., 401(k) or 403(b), you should take advantage of this. But, don't consider these plans the end-all be-all. Why? While it may appear to be free money, the taxation on the harvest is much more detrimental than the tax on the seed would be. In other words, it is better to take your

---

[53] National Center For Retirement Benefits, Inc., "30 Serious Errors and Problems Found in Pension and Profit Sharing Plans," NCRB, http://www.ncrb.com/errors.html [accessed January 30, 2008].

tax lump in the beginning than at the end, when you retire. And since the 401(k) is taxed at the end, you're paying taxes on a much larger amount than you would if you got taxed at the beginning of your investments.

Profit sharing plans or stock bonus plans. A profit sharing or stock bonus plan is a defined contribution plan that provides a formula for allocating portions of annual contributions to each employee. These plans can include 401(k)s, and the employer or employee determines how much will be put into the plan.

Fully insured defined benefit plans. These plans [formerly referred to as 412(i) plans] run on the same chassis as a traditional defined benefit plan. These plans must utilize fixed products guaranteed by an insurance carrier, such as fixed annuities and whole life insurance. Because a fully insured plan uses guaranteed rates of return, the contributions tend to be higher than in a traditional defined benefit plan that uses an actuarial assumption of 5.5 percent.

These plans have fixed annual contributions that must be made for a minimum of five years to satisfy IRS permanency issues. Any interest earned in the plan that exceeds the guaranteed minimum will be used to reduce future contributions. The trend in fully insured plans is for the contribution to reduce as the years go on, creating less cost for the same benefit.

Traditional IRA. If your income level is too high for you to start or continue contributing to a Roth IRA (see below), you can still make a contribution to a traditional IRA. The contribution limits are the same as for the Roth, and those limits apply to total annual IRA contributions; in other words, you can't contribute $4,000 to a Roth and $4,000 to a traditional IRA (at least until contribution limits reach $8,000 a year).

A traditional IRA grows tax-deferred and is taxed as ordinary income upon withdrawal—not the best way to do things. Contributions are tax-deductible if 1) your employer doesn't offer a retirement plan, or 2) your adjusted gross income is below a certain level. Those levels change every year, so check with your tax preparer or financial planner. For 2007, for example, the limit was $50,000 (gradually phased out until $60,000) for single tax filers or $80,000 (gradually phased out until $100,000) for married filers.

Roth IRA. This type of IRA is great in that you get taxed on the money you put into the plan rather than on the money that accumulates in it, which, as we've discussed, is a much larger amount, since it grows over time. That tax-free growth is one of the great benefits of the Roth. It allows you to reap the earnings without paying taxes on them.

Also, Roth IRAs provide a great amount of control to the individual investor because you can open them through a broker rather than through an employee-sponsored plan. This allows you to direct the investments into individual securities. If you like a particular stock, you have the freedom to direct funds from your Roth into that stock.

Now, most IRAs and employee-sponsored plans force you to start taking distributions of the money you've accumulated by April of the year after you turn seventy years and six months old. For most people, that's fine, since by then, most of us are retired and in need of the income. But some people would rather wait to take the money out so that it has a chance to enjoy more tax-free growth. The Roth IRA carries no mandatory distributions and so allows those people to leave the money in the fund.[54]

Roth IRAs are not open to everyone. Income restrictions mean that the contribution limits begin to kick in at a modified adjusted gross income of $99,000 for single filers and $156,000 for joint filers, reaching the ineligible stage at $114,000 and $166,000, respectively. The contribution limit for a Roth (and traditional IRA as well) is $4,000 for 2005 through 2007, and $5,000 for 2008. Thereafter, the $5,000 maximum allowable contribution will be indexed to inflation in $500 increments. This does not really offer much in terms of a significant build-up if you're getting a late start in life.

---

[54] Robert Brokamp, "Where to Invest Your Money," The Motley Fool, http://www.fool.com/retirement/retirement02.htm [accessed December 26, 2007].

Taxes on Deferred Pension Plans

As we've already discussed, the payments you receive from your retirement funds will be taxed as regular income when you retire. Not only that, but the income from your retirement fund will be added to any other income you might be earning in your retirement years. This can often push you into a higher tax bracket than the one you fell into during your working years. Some people are trying to avoid this by waiting until they're required to take their mandatory distributions. As we discussed above, this strategy is employed when people believe they might "spend down" their other income first.[55]

When you consider that your withdrawals must be large enough to cover your expenses plus the taxes on the withdrawals, finding yourself in a higher bracket isn't as unlikely as you might think—especially when you consider that up to eighty-five percent of your Social Security benefits can become taxable if your income, over and above those benefits, exceeds certain thresholds.

The news is even worse if you want to withdraw all of your money at once. If your plan is worth anything, you'll definitely be penalized with huge taxes. There is one exception to this: If you were born before 1936, you can use what's called the "ten-year averaging option" to reduce the tax hit you'll take. This method still requires that you pay taxes, but the tax bracket you fall into will be calculated as though you'd taken out the money over a ten-year period. That's pretty handy, because it helps you avoid getting pushed into a higher tax bracket because of your withdrawals.

Mandatory Distributions

Once you're required to take distributions from your retirement account, there will be a minimum amount you have to take out each year; that sum will be determined by the IRS. If you don't take these distributions, you'll be panelized.

You can figure out how much you'll have to take in distributions by dividing your retirement account's balance prior to receiving dis-

---

[55] Precision Information, LLC, "Ordinary Income Taxes on Retirement Plan Distributions," New York Life, http://www.newyorklife.com/cda/0,3254,11531,00.html [accessed December 26, 2007].

tributions by the distribution period found in the IRS' uniform lifetime table guide. The distribution period is a little strange in that it's determined by the joint life expectancy of you and an imaginary beneficiary ten years younger than you are.

Now, if your spouse is your sole beneficiary, the distribution is based on your actual life expectancies. That is if he or she is ten years younger than you are. The result of calculating life expectancy with someone younger than you is usually of benefit to you in that this method typically lowers the required distribution.[56] The shorter your combined life expectancies, the larger the required distributions.

Based on the current taxation scheme the government has created with respect to pension plans, the average retired couple will pay eight to twelve times more in taxes on their IRAs and 401(k)s during their retirement years than they saved during their contribution and accumulation years, because their money has grown so much during their working years. This is one of the reasons I'm such a proponent of paying taxes up front.

An article in *U.S. News and World Report* in 2006 came to the same conclusion, and stated, "It may be better to pay tax now on retirement savings."[57] Paying taxes now, rather than waiting until you make withdrawals, can especially benefit people who end up in a higher tax bracket when they retire. Young people in a low tax bracket in the early stages of their careers may get only a modest kick from a traditional 401(k) compared with the future tax-free income from a Roth 401(k), or if they got the triple compound by using properly structured life insurance and could use the cash values tax-free.

I think we can count on tax rates going up in the near future, since we know that the lower tax rates on dividends, capital gains and ordinary income are all set to expire at the end of 2010. At the time of this writing, we are going into another presidential race where Americans disfavor GOP politics and would like a change. A new Democratic regime would be looking for a way to deal with

---

[56] "Taxes on Retirement Plan Distributions Taken after age 70 ½" New York Life, http://www.newyorklife.com/cda/0,3254,11540,00.html [January 28, 2008].
[57] Leonard Wiener, "It may be better to pay tax now on retirement savings," U.S. News & World Report, July 18, 2006.

Social Security and Medicare benefits, since much of our population is aging. Therefore, any politician who wants to be elected will have to give it to them.

John Edwards, for example, released a tax plan during his campaign that called for raising the top tax rate on long-term capital gains from fifteen to twenty-eight percent, as well as for repealing favorable tax rates on all types of income for those earning more than $200,000. Consistent with its intention to support low-income families, the plan also includes a small tax exemption on the first $250 of investment income, to encourage those of modest means to start saving and investing. What a guy.

Tax Penalties on Retirement Withdrawals

In general, money cannot be withdrawn from traditional IRAs or 401(k)/403(b) plans prior to age fifty-nine and a half without incurring a ten-percent penalty.

However, IRS Publication 575, "Pension and Annuity Income," tells us that an early distribution penalty will not apply when withdrawals are made "from a qualified retirement (other than an IRA) after your separation from service in or after the year in which you reached age fifty-five."[58] Therefore, when you leave your job in or after the year of your fifty-fifth birthday, you may take money from your employer's retirement plan(s) and only have to worry about paying ordinary income taxes. Exceptions are explained in Section 72(t) of the Internal Revenue Code.

In addition, a substantially equal periodic payment plan, or SEPP, may be used at any age to avoid the early withdrawal penalties. The rules permit distributions "made as part of a series of substantially equal periodic payments (made at least annually) for your life (or life expectancy) or the joint lives (or joint life expectancies) of you and your beneficiary (but, if from a qualified retirement plan other than an IRA, only if the payments begin after your separation from service)."[59]

---

[58] Department of the Treasury Internal Revenue Service, "Pension and Annuity Income," Internal Revenue Service, http://www.irs.gov/pub/irs-pdf/p575.pdf [December 26, 2007], 30-40.
[59] Department of the Treasury Internal Revenue Service, "401(k) Resource Guide – Plan Participants—General Distribution Rules," Internal Revenue Service, http://www.irs.gov/retirement/participant/article/0,,id=151787,00.html, [January 28, 2008].

Basically, you can start taking money from your retirement plan before the age of fifty-nine and a half, without paying taxes or a penalty, if you agree to take the money in the form of payments over a minimum of five years. The IRS allows three methods for taking SEPP, and each method results in a different amount that must be taken each year.

Income In Respect of Decedent (IRD)

Income in respect of decedent (IRD) is considered one of the bloodiest thorns on the wealth transfer rose. In order to prevent the bunching of all income received after a decedent's death on the final income tax return, Congress enacted this concept, which essentially provides for taxing the beneficiary on the postmortem income as it is received. There is no all-purpose definition of IRD found in the tax code. Treasury Regulations section 1.691(a-b) provides a general guideline, saying that IRD includes "those amounts to which a decedent was entitled as gross income but which were not properly includable in computing taxable income for the taxable year ending with the date of his death."[60]

IRD is taxed at the same levels as it would have been had it gone to the decedent, and is excluded from the step-up or step-down in basis usually received on property when it is valued at fair market value upon the death of the owner, because it hasn't gone on their income tax return. It is, however includible in the decedent's estate tax return.[61]

To avoid the IRD, the beneficiary has to show that the property wouldn't have been part of the decedent's gross income when it was received—for instance, Roth IRA distributions. Likewise, properly structured life insurance would avoid this. IRD coupled with estate tax can eliminate seventy-five percent of the assets or seventy-five cents on every dollar left to a beneficiary.

IRD is insidious and can wipe out much of the value of the property left to a beneficiary. The typical result of IRD is that the

---

[60] Internal Revenue Code of the United States Code, Section 691 and Treasury Regulations section 1.691(a-b).
[61] Debra H. Oden and Ben Sutherland, "Maximizing the Tax Deduction for Income in Respect of a Decedent," The CPA Journal, September 2005, http://www.nysscpa.org/cpa-journal/2005/905/essentials/p40.htm [December 26, 2007].

beneficiary is left with $27,000 (or less) for each $100,000 of plan funds subjected to IRD. That can leave even a $1 million plan with a worth of just $330,000 when combined with income and estate taxes.

As you can see, planning has its advantages, and there are millions of Americans with IRAs and pension plans out there who have close to this dollar amount in them or more. You cannot win this game just by taking distributions during your lifetime.

The solution to this situation rests in what we call the IRDEP™ or an IRD elimination plan. This is simply done but purchasing an immediate annuity, payable for life, that is income-tax-free and has no value at death, so there is no estate tax. You would then fund a wealth-creation trust with life insurance, which is further outside the estate and not subjected to the estate tax. There may be other strategies unique to your circumstances, so there is no replacement for great planning.

Qualified Versus Non-qualified Plans

I'm often asked what the difference is between qualified and non-qualified plans, and I think it is important to explain it by example, since most tax preparers look at the pre-tax dollar aspect of a qualified plan rather than at the overall picture. As you know, I prefer that my clients be taxed on their contributions rather than their distributions, which runs contrary to the conventional tax preparer way of thinking.

Qualified

Sam, age forty, wishes to retire at age sixty-five. He is in the thirty-percent tax bracket and deposits into an investment $30,000 per year for thirty years, at seven percent interest, equaling $2,193,117 by the time he retires.

Sam is invested in a tax-deferred savings vehicle that gives him a tax break on the money he puts into the investment. Vehicles like these, including IRAs, allow you deduct your contributions from your gross income, thereby easing your tax burden during your working years. He receives an approximate annual tax savings of about $9,000, for a total tax savings of $225,000 during his working years. Sam would receive a "net" retirement income of $135,430 per year, assuming a thirty percent tax bracket because he receives no tax break when withdrawing the money from his retirement account. His money would last for just eleven years after taxes. He could take less per year and extend his dollars, but the point is, he is going to be hammered at ordinary income tax rates, which are going up right now.

Sam would end up paying over $638,454 on his retirement income at the thirty-percent level. It just doesn't make sense to take the tax breaks during your working years, when you've got a steady income. Sam's total net retirement income after taxes is $1,554,660—not the most efficient way to save for retirement.

Non-qualified

Jim, who is the same age as Sam, deposits $30,000 per year until the age of sixty-five, assuming an eight percent return. Jim receives NO tax savings on his deposits. He receives a "net" retirement income of $211,712 per year until the age of ninety-five, without taxes. Jim's total taxes paid on retirement income equal zero dollars. His total net retirement income after taxes is more than $6,351,360. Following Jim's plan would involve using a tax-deferred life insurance vehicle, but it is possible, and it offers fantastic tax benefits.

The Difference

The taxes Sam saved on his deposits total $225,000 on the qualified plan and zero dollars on the non-qualified plan. However, the taxes he pays on his retirement income total $638,454 on the qualified plan, compared to the zero dollars Jim paid on the non-qualified plan. That equals a tax savings of over $1,230,000.

That's a total net income paid of $2,193,117 on the qualified plan, and $6,351,360 paid on the non-qualified plan. That's a difference of $6,100,000. I'd say that would make a big difference in the lifestyle you could enjoy during retirement.

Overall Difference of $4,158,247

Can you afford to lose this type of opportunity just to save a few dollars on taxes each year? The non-qualified plan would have an initial death benefit of over $2,000,000, in case Jim was to pass away early. You'll have to be the judge, but the smart approach to the money would be looking at the end game. It truly is better to be taxed on the seed than the harvest. Perhaps the best solution is to use both and spend down the least efficient dollars first; these are the qualified plan dollars, which are subject to ordinary income tax. Then, use the nontaxable funds that are created with a non-qualified strategy.

College Planning

The vehicle of choice for college planning seems to be the 529 plan, but I don't think it is the best way. These plans totaled almost $97 billion at the end of the first quarter of 2007, up thirty percent compared with the same period in 2006, according to the College Savings Foundation. If you rely too heavily on 529s, you could end up with more money in the accounts than you have to pay in qualified college costs, which would trigger the very tax you were trying to avoid. Once dollars are placed in a 529 plan for education, that's all they can be used for without being subject to a horrendous tax and penalty.

I have seen people buy investment real estate when their kids are young, allow the kids to take out student loans throughout college, earning a credit rating, and then in one fell swoop, sell the property and pay off the loan. The kids then have no debt from college, but they walk away with having taken out a student loan and completely paid it off.

Another strategy relies on using life insurance. Why? Because it is one of the assets that is not considered when determining scholarship and other financial aid eligibility. What if you had a big, maxed-out 529 plan and your kid got a scholarship? You couldn't get that money out for any other purpose besides education without paying the taxes and penalty on it. You've just imprisoned your dollars.

What if we have another geopolitical event like 9/11, and it is time for your child to start college? Since most if not all of the 529 plans are invested in equity funds without market protection, the dollars are vulnerable to this type of world event, and would likely be down fifty percent.

The right answer is probably to consider funding several options. That is, do a small 529 plan so that you don't overfund it; think about purchasing investment property that you could sell as a partial 1031 exchange (avoiding capital gains); and put away money in a non-qualified plan so that you have proceeds to pay for college that are not scrutinized for financial aid eligibility. In addition, a properly funded index life insurance strategy can kick the pants off the 529 plan because it reduces those pernicious expenses, reduces the taxes and leaves a death benefit.

What We Learned

1. There is no more trustworthiness in corporate pension plans.

2. In 2005, underfunding of plans increased to nearly $182 billion.

3. Determine which plan works best for your situation.

4. Does your employer match you dollar for dollar?

5. When you retire, the payments you receive from ordinary retirement funds are taxed at regular income tax rates upon withdrawal.

6. Paying tax now rather than waiting until you make withdrawals can especially benefit people who end up in a higher tax bracket when they retire.

7. The beneficiary of an estate that includes a retirement plan is left with $27,000 (or less) for each $100,000 of plan funds subjected to IRD.

8. Once dollars are placed in a 529 plan for education, that's all they can be used for without being subjected to horrific tax.

9. There are alternatives to funding a college education beyond a 529 plan.

CHAPTER FOURTEEN

Self-directed Pension Plans

If you have any money in an IRA, you are among only forty-one percent of American households that do. The mean balance of IRA assets in those households is less than $50,000 and in recent history, personal savings rates have decreased. The polls and statistics show that Americans spend more than they save, and that, combined with a general decline in personal savings, is serving to harm the long-term wealth accumulation of millions of Americans.

In order to help avoid some of the typical retirement planning mistakes people make, I'll use this chapter to focus on the steps you can take to wrest control of your pension planning from financial advisors who have only their own retirement interests at heart.

This chapter is in conjunction with the last chapter and is designed to inform you that you have choices—many choices—in terms of your investment vehicles. The majority of IRA sponsors, including banks, brokerage firms and insurance companies, limit your investment options to the financial products that benefit them the most. This is usually mutual funds, although it could be individual stocks, and finding success with those is like looking for a needle in a haystack.

A Little History
The concept of self-directed investing was first introduced in 1974, when the Employee

Retirement and Income Savings Act, also known as ERISA, was passed. Through ERISA the IRA and 401k were created and the responsibility for retirement investing was passed from the employer to the individual, creating the ability to self-direct investments.

The problem is that most people have no idea that they can utilize their retirement accounts to purchase investments other than the traditional stocks, bonds, mutual funds or money market accounts that most people use. In fact, nearly all of the $10 trillion invested in retirement accounts in the United States is still held in these types of investments, since the brokerage firms have no real incentive to educate you on self-directed investing.

If investors had been advised that they could use their retirement funds to invest in non-traditional investments, like real estate, instead of remaining stuck in the stock market witnessing continued losses over the last few years, many informed investors would have abandoned this losing approach to wealth building.

Investment Options

You have choices and alternatives in directing the investments in your IRA or pension plan, and the choices are several and varied. The self-directed IRA has the same rules as a traditional IRA in that the money cannot be withdrawn prior to age fifty-nine without a penalty; it is also eligible for substantially equal periodic payments (Rev. Ruling 2002-62 allows one-time modification); and it abides by other exceptions, including medical, educational and first-time home purchase. The benefit, though, is that you don't have to remain tied to losses in the market and the likely bad management of a fund that is out of your control.

The IRS allows a wide range of investment options in your retirement plan, and self-directed accounts allow every type of investment for your maximum independent wealth accumulation. It's important that you educate yourself about those options and understand what's happening with the money you'll depend on when you retire. Following are some definitions you should become familiar with.

Prohibited Transactions and Investments

Being ignorant of what prohibited transactions are can wreak havoc on your IRA. If you get these wrong, you can nullify the tax-exempt status of your IRA and land yourself some large fines to boot. Become familiar with the following definitions to help keep yourself out of trouble.

Prohibited Investments

Rather than providing a list of the investments you can make inside of an IRA, the Internal Revenue Code lists what you cannot invest in. The list is fairly extensive but mostly focuses on personal property. Things like artwork, coins and gems are prohibited and unfortunately, so is life insurance. Make sure you talk to your financial advisor before directing your IRA into any investments so that you can make sure to avoid anything prohibited.

Prohibited Transactions

The IRS defines a prohibited transaction as follows: "Generally a prohibited transaction is any improper use of your IRA account or annuity by you, your beneficiary or any disqualified person. Disqualified persons include your fiduciary and members of your family (spouse, ancestor, linear descendant, and any spouse of linear descendant)."[62]

If you've noticed that the list of prohibited individuals includes you, then you're on the right track to understanding that IRAs are trusts. They are not personal bank accounts. That means that you cannot personally benefit from an investment made by your IRA. I know you're probably thinking, *But my IRA is designed to build wealth for my retirement.* That is true. But the IRC dictates that your IRA cannot buy property from you. So, you couldn't direct your IRA to purchase your home. However, traditional IRAs can sell to and buy from brothers, sisters, aunts, uncles, cousins, nieces, nephews and step relatives. Roth IRAs cannot.[63]

---

[62] Internal Revenue Service, IRS Publication 590, 40-41.
[63] Equity Trust Company, "Prohibited IRA Transactions," Equity Trust Company, http://www.trustetc.com/investment/prohibited-ira-transactions.html [December 27, 2007].

Now, when someone does violate the rules and involves a prohibited person in a transaction, it's called "self-dealing." The reason behind this circular logic of having an IRA not benefit you is that IRAs are viewed as being for your retirement, not for a financial windfall right now.

Handling Your IRA

When investing in a self-directed IRA or pension plan, remember that not all companies will offer you consultation and advice. A lot of companies merely execute the investments you want made and leave the rest to you. If you're uncomfortable with being in total control of your investments, you're going to want to find a company that offers you some assistance.

Once you've found a company that offers the savings plan that fits you best, you're going to want to consider forming a limited liability company, which will offer protection to you during any investments you make through a self-directed IRA or other pension plan. It also allows the owner of the IRA to write checks directly from the IRA, to cover expenses related to the investments. This holds true for real estate expenses as well.

Remember, though, that when using your self-directed IRA to pay for these expenses, it should be done through checks and should conform to all laws and regulations related to this kind of expenditure. Paying out of pocket can leave you vulnerable to tax liabilities.

Buying Real Property With Loans

If debt or financing is used by an IRA (or a partnership, or an LLC in which an IRA invests) to make an investment, the income generated by the portion of the investment that was financed is unrelated debt-financed income (UDFI).

UDFI is the proportionate share of income generated by rents collected (net of deductions such as mortgage interest, property taxes and ordinary operating expenses), as well as any capital gains realized if the property is sold. In particular, the portion of the income that is subject to UDFI would be the amount of the purchase price that is financed. As the debt is paid down, the portion of income that is UDFI decreases proportionally. Any income realized at least twelve months after the debt is fully paid is not UDFI.

Unrelated Business Taxable Income (UBTI)

The unrelated business taxable income rule was enacted in 1950 to keep tax-exempt businesses from competing with non-tax exempt companies by taxing any activities that went against their stated purpose. Since an IRA is tax-deferred, and therefore exempt,[64] any income derived from a business owned or operated by the IRA will be subject to UBIT if it produces a profit.[65]

If you use your IRA to start a business or LLC that purchases a moneymaking entity, such as a rental property, you'll be taxed on any profits. Moreover, each time debt is used by a tax-deferred or tax-exempt entity (with some exceptions), tax is applied to that portion of the gain that is debt-financed. This income is called "unrelated debt financed income," or UDFI, which is related to UBTI. Taxes on both are calculated and reported on IRS form 990-T.

If you're uncertain about whether your property will be considered debt-financed, just know that any property held to produce income is debt-financed property if at any time during the tax year there was money owed on the property. When that property is owned by a tax-exempt entity, then taxes will apply. The amount of the tax liability will be determined by examining how much was owed on the property during the time it was held by the tax-exempt organization.

Make sure you understand the tax implications of buying a profit-producing property or investment through your tax-exempt organization. There are formulas for calculating acquisition debt and other related expenses you'll need to understand your tax liabilities, but suffice to say that you should have a good tax attorney when getting involved in complex investments.

---

[64] Internal Revenue Code of the United States Code, Section 408(e)(1).
[65] Internal Revenue Code of the United States Code, Section 511.

Solo Roth

The Solo Roth is a relatively new retirement option that allows an individual or married couple who own their own business to sock away up to $98,000 per year for retirement. Of this amount, $40,000 can be composed of after-tax Roth elective contributions, if all eligible parties are over fifty.

The Solo Roth offers huge potential for business owners who have no employees other than their spouses, in that it provides tax-free growth on a much larger amount than is available through a normal Roth IRA; in fact, it's five times as much. In addition, there are no income restrictions on the Solo Roth, which means you're not ineligible if you make more than $110,000 as an individual or $160,000 if married and filing jointly. There is another benefit to Solo Roth 401(k)s. They are allowed to put money into two investments that are prohibited under a normal Roth IRA. A Solo Roth 401(k) can invest in an S corporation stock and life insurance. Additionally, unlike IRAs, where you cannot take out a loan, according to Pensco Trust Company, you can personally borrow up to $50,000 or fifty percent (lesser of the two) from your Solo Roth 401(k).[66] That provides a cash flow opportunity that a Roth IRA cannot provide.

To better understand what your contribution would look like if you were a business owner and had a Solo Roth 401(k), let's look at an example. If you earned $100,000 in a given year from your business or sole proprietorship, your maximum 401(k) contribution to a traditional IRA would be $20,000. But with a Solo, you could contribute $15,500 in salary deferrals, and up to twenty percent of what you earned, which would be $20,000. So, you could contribute $35,500, a nice sum when planning for retirement.[67]

Therefore, as a self-employed business owner with no employees other than your spouse, a solo Roth 401(k) allows you to put away more money for tax-free growth on your earnings.[68]

---
[66] Pensco Trust Company, "Finally, a Marriage of Two of the Most Popular Plans," Pensco Trust Company,
http://www.penscotrust.com/education/solo_roth_401k_and_solo_401k.asp [January 15, 2008].
[67] Elizabeth Carlassare, host, "The Solo 401(k)," MoneyGirl, March 13, 2007,
http://moneygirl.quickanddirtytips.com/solo-401k.aspx [January 15, 2008].
[69] Carlassare, http://moneygirl.quickanddirtytips.com/solo-401k.aspx.

Also, a Solo Roth 401(k) offers the opportunity to invest in real estate, even through the use of debt financing, without facing the tax penalties you'd face with a traditional IRA. I've seen many clients of mine put down $500 in the morning on a real estate purchase and flip the purchase contract in the afternoon without paying any tax on the gains. The new gains would be tax-deferred thereafter, if they had been funded by the tax-deferred components of the Solo 401(k), or tax-free if funded by the elective Roth component.[69]

There are a lot of intricacies involved in self-directing your pension. You need to get educated and work with someone who can advise you on a couple of your creative transactions before you pull the trigger, but the benefits can be immense.

What We Learned

1. The majority of IRA sponsors limit your investment options to expensive financial products.

2. The IRS allows a wide range of investment options in your retirement plan, and self-directed accounts allow every type of investment, for your maximum independent wealth accumulation.

3. Understanding what constitutes a prohibited transaction is very important when it comes to making investments within your self-directed IRA.

4. Companies that offer self-directed IRAs and pension plans can vary significantly in how much assistance they give to their clients.

---

[69] Carlassare, http://moneygirl.quickanddirtytips.com/solo-401k.aspx.

5. A Solo Roth 401(k) will allow an individual, or a married couple who own their own business, to sock away up to $98,000 per year for retirement.

6. The Roth Solo 401(k) allows for contributions five times greater than a Roth IRA and has no cap on the amount of income an individual can earn before he or she becomes ineligible to contribute.

CHAPTER FIFTEEN

Running Your Family Finances Like a Business

I want to start off by telling you that running your family like a business isn't as bad as it might sound. I don't want you getting hardcore and going too far with this, but a family should employ a few of the practices that a business would use, like budgeting and doing a monthly cash flow management to check on its investments and measure its liabilities. This process is just to better understand what your family's finances are doing and where you're headed.

Cash flow management is the process of monitoring, analyzing and adjusting your business' cash flows, and in the family setting, adjusting your lifestyle cash flows. It's like a visit to the doctor for your finances, to make sure everything is okay.

When I first introduced this idea to my wife, she said, "No way. You're not turning our family into a business and controlling us." I was able to convince her, though, that the process would allow her to have more spending money if we were able to track our spending and cut costs from unnecessary expenditures. That worked. We now have a family board meeting monthly, and my son even participates.

If you think you're the breadwinning professional male and you know it all, think again. I get some compelling feedback from my wife and my son, from places my mind is just not trained to go anymore, and it helps solve problems. It's also a way for my family to spend time together, and it can do the same for yours. I know it doesn't sound that fun but when you're planning annual meetings in destinations like Hawaii or Costa Rica, it takes on a different complexion. And, the extra money you find in your finances can help you do that.

I know that looking at your finances isn't the most exciting thing in the world, and for some families, it can even cause tension. But I assure you that if you're not paying attention, no one else is, either.

What I've seen with some of my clients is that they do a little act that I call "ostriching," which means that they plant their heads in the sand and never look up to see what their finances are doing. I had one client who bought more than eight rental properties and didn't track them to see what they were doing, or how much they were costing him on a monthly basis. He had also bought these properties through a vendor who retailed them at the top of the market, so that when things changed, guess what happened? That's right—they started being a real expense and when they weren't rented, a serious threat to the integrity of my client's wealth accumulation.

Hiding from the truth won't make it go away. My client didn't pay attention to what was happening with his money, and as a consequence, he paid the price, literally and figuratively.

The most common concern for a business is controlling its cash flow, and it makes sense to use some of this thinking in your personal finances. Would you buy your family operation right now, based on the balance sheet? How does your cash flow look? No, really, I want you to look at this. Is there more debt that cash flow?

For small businesses, the most important aspect of cash flow management is avoiding extended cash shortages, caused by having too great a gap between cash inflows and outflows. You won't be able to stay in business if you can't pay your bills for any extended length of time. How can you expect to be in the business of providing for a family, saving for college and then managing a future retirement fund if you don't fundamentally control your cash flow?

If you've fallen into the trillion-dollar debt pit like millions of Americans, you need to analyze your cash flow on a regular basis, and use cash flow forecasting so you can take the steps necessary to head off further cash flow problems. Many software accounting programs have built-in reporting features that make cash flow analysis easy. This is the first step of cash flow management.

I mentioned http://www.debtmd.com in a prior chapter; this site is fantastic, and you can use its services for free, even though many companies are selling software for $3,500 and more to do the same thing. I have personally used this site to bail me out of a few traps, and it really works.

In order to have a realistic chance at building wealth, you need to take steps to shorten your cash flow conversion period, so that your family finances can bring in money faster. These steps may include:

1) Monitoring your use of credit and adjusting your credit limits accordingly. By tracking your spending habits, you'll get an idea of where you spend your money. By evaluating the results, you can see if you're using money for things that aren't really necessary. For example, do you have a gym membership you pay monthly, even though you never go to the gym? Do you buy coffee every morning (special brand) when it's available in your home for less, or your office for free? Look at all the places where you can save money; even small outlays can add up.

1. Establishing a deposit policy for savings and investments. This means deploying funds into a separate holding account for the express purpose of saving money and investing it. This isn't an account you dip into when you want that new pair of shoes you saw at the mall.

2. Tracking your past-due accounts and actively paying them down with a payment strategy you can create at http://www.debtmd.com, or by using other software, such as Money™.

3. Consider paying yourself first. This idea is not new, but it's a strategy that starts a consistent savings program. Unless your entire paycheck is earmarked for monthly bills and necessities, you should be able to put money into an investment every month. This is another reason why equity

management needs to be examined. If too much of your paycheck is going toward a mortgage, you might be in the wrong home for your budget. If you don't think you'll be in the home for the rest of your life, explore lowering the payments and putting that savings away.

4. Take a hard look at that company retirement plan. Not all plans are created equal. If your employer is not matching you dollar-for-dollar, it might not be that great of a plan and you should probably not put a ton of your income into it. Remember that money is only deferred from being taxed. You have to pay the piper one day at ordinary income tax levels and in a potentially higher bracket if your income increases as you advance in your career.

5. Do you buy impulsively? In other words, do you buy without checking your finances first and doing a real assessment of your need for an item? While we should not let our finances stand in the way of our progress and improving our lives, you need to remember, before you buy another consumer good with a credit card, that the card was originally designed for traveling salesmen, for expenses that were deductible. Your new designer duds may not be deductible or have a business purpose, and that means you're going to pay full price plus interest. This is not to say that you shouldn't have fun or treat yourself. I just want you to create a positive cash flow beforehand that allows you never to fall behind. Once you have a few investments in play, then you can have the freedom to spend more lavishly; until then, you have a mission to accomplish and that is to get yourself right with your personal finances.

Balancing Your Spending

It's important for you to learn how to budget your money. Now, various people have proffered differing ratios as the best way to allocate your income when trying to minimize debt. I personally think that each situation is unique and requires a plan based on your needs at the time. But, there are some general outlines I think are good to follow.

You should spend the majority of your income on living expenses—perhaps two thirds or more. At the same time, really examine what your expenses are and if there are opportunities to pare them down.

Put about twenty percent of your money toward an investment. These are the investments that will carry you through retirement, so take this seriously. If you have debts, use a portion of this twenty percent to pay those off as well. Debt will weigh you down, unless it's debt you've used to create more income. So, car payments, credit cards and other expenses need to be taken care of.

The last portion of your income might be the most important. This is going to go toward an "emergency" fund—everyone should have one. Saving money specifically for unexpected expenses will save you more trouble than you can imagine. Too often, people are put under by a seemingly small expense, like a car repair or medical procedure. Just a few thousand dollars can cause serious harm to your financial situation, and it's important to prepare for that eventuality.

Now, you're probably asking, "Where's the fun? When do I get to use my money for something fun?" Everyone should have fun, and there's nothing wrong with buying new things for yourself. Set aside a small portion of your income, maybe five percent, for the things you want to buy—a new car, a nice watch, a new TV.

I hope these guidelines help. Remember, though, that you need to examine your own situation and adjust to it. If you have an unusual amount of debts, you might want to allocate more money for paying those down.

Personal Budget and Finding Your Cash Flow

In Chapter Nine, we discussed what cash flow is and how it affects your family's budget. Now is the time to use what you've found out about your cash flow and create a personal budget for you and your family.

If you haven't already calculated your cash flow, then do so now, using a month-long period as a benchmark. Remember to only include income that is earned or expended on a regular basis. You don't want any unusual or one-time income to throw your numbers off.

Once you have a budget laid out for each month, you'll be able to start identifying ways to either save more money or earn more money—the point being to improve your net, positive cash flow. While this seems very simple on its face, I know it is not that easy. Some people, though, don't even acknowledge their situation and get deeper in the hole. Remember, hope is not an investment strategy. You cannot ignore your situation and hope that it improves. That's right—this is up to YOU to do.

Although the point of this chapter has not been a credit-counseling message, it is in line with the message I've been trying to get across to you. Fiscal responsibility is the reason why only a handful of people can be wealthy and successful. Some people come up with a great idea and build a business, while the millionaire next door just plods along and looks at his or her numbers, has some guts, makes a decision or two on an investment and still reaches the same destination. The difference between that millionaire and you is likely a few small choices, and a dedication to financial understanding and vigilance. Don't be afraid to make changes based on what you find with your finances. Include in your thought process the possibility of owning your own business.

The Beauty of Business Ownership

If you don't own a business outside of your primary employment, you might want to think about starting one. If you feel comfortable examining your family's cash flow and you've become accustomed to operating a business-style budget, the next reasonable step may be to start a business. The tax benefits of doing so are substantial; if you start a business and lose some money in your first year of operation, you can at least reap many of the tax benefits, including the ability to deduct your expenses from your adjusted gross income (AGI).

Once you own just one investment property, you can incorporate and create a business.

In short, expenses incurred by a business are tax-deductible. This federal credit allows businesses (and business owners) to offset their tax liabilities by the amount of expenses paid. For example: If, in the first year of your business, you have gross sales of $10,000, and your expenses for starting and running your business during that year total $25,000, your net income is a loss. But, because of the loss, the federal government will allow you to gain some credit for the financial outlay in getting started—and then some.

If you start running your business on the side and still have a salary from your primary employer, where you are only getting standard deductions, you can offset that primary income with the losses from your business. Let's assume for practical purposes that you are earning $75,000 annually. Keeping it simple, let's say you fall into the thirty-percent tax bracket. This means that on average, your tax liability is $22,500 (thirty percent of $75,000). That's a lot of your hard-earned money going to Uncle Sam.

When you use certain types of corporations, though, your net revenue (gross sales minus expenses) is a straight-line entry on your personal federal tax return. This entry directly affects your adjusted gross income. Your AGI is increased if your business was profitable and made money, but your AGI is decreased if your business was not profitable (expenses were greater than income). Because the example above shows a loss, you would put $7500 back into your pocket—a gift from Uncle Sam for starting your own business. Obviously, you'd have preferred that your business be profitable, but our example shows that being a business owner offers tax benefits that working as an employee doesn't. Starting a business is something to consider once you've got a handle on understanding and tracking cash flow.

If you're thinking about starting a business, take some time to understand the tax laws associated with it. When you start your business, it will have to eventually become profitable or the IRS will claim you have a hobby. You usually have to show a profit for three years in a five-year period to keep the IRS at bay, but there are other ways to prove that you're truly running a business. If you can show that you're putting in the time and effort it takes to make the business profitable, and that your losses are beyond your control, you should be able to avoid undue scrutiny. There are other allowances made by the IRS, so make sure you're familiar with the regulations that affect your business.

When Amazon.com started, they said in their business plan that they did not intend to make a profit for twenty years. When you provide in your business plan that you intend to make a profit but that current market factors will prevent this for an extended period of time, you have a good argument showing that you are on track, but that ordinary factors will continue to prevent your profitability. The lesson in this is, you should try to be profitable and not simply go after the tax deductions alone, which is why real estate investing makes sense. If you don't stay within the rules, you could get an audit, which is a waste of time and money, since you will have to spend time fighting the IRS and paying an accountant, instead of focusing on making money.

There are five things that will prevent you from accumulating wealth and two of them have been discussed in this chapter: taxes and debt. You can take control of both of these factors by creating a debt-reduction plan and starting a side business to offset taxes with either deductions or potential losses your first couple of years with the business.

What We Learned

1. Cash flow management is the process of monitoring, analyzing and adjusting your lifestyle cash flows.

2. The most important aspect of cash flow management is avoiding extended cash shortages, caused by having too great a gap between cash inflows and outflows.

3. Consider using http://www.debtmd.com to create a payment strategy to reduce your outflows.

4. There are five steps to shorten cash flow conversion:
    a. Monitor your use of credit and adjust credit limits.
    a. Establish a deposit policy for savings and investments.
    a. Track past-due accounts and actively pursue paying them down.
    a. Pay yourself first; you should be able to put money into an investment every month.
    a. Take a hard look at that company retirement plan and deciding whether it makes sense to be taxed when you retire and the sum is large, or when it is small and placed in other assets for uninterrupted growth and use.

5. The seventy-twenty-ten rule:
    a. Spend seventy percent on living expenses.
    a. Save twenty percent and put it into an investment or debt management.
    a. Save five percent for an emergency cash fund.
    a. Save five percent for specific goals.

4. Budget and find your personal cash flow with the formula provided.

4. Starting a legitimate home business may be a great thing for you.

CHAPTER SIXTEEN

How Mortgage Management Can Create Wealth

Managing your mortgage does not mean simply paying it off early. I hope that I've proved to you in previous chapters that simply paying off debts early will not provide for you and your family when you retire. You need to accumulate assets, and your mortgage can help you do that.

You are living in a time that offers some of the best opportunities to use the Three Secret Pillars of Wealth! And even if you're not in the super-wealthy club, where you can trade assets while looking for the arbitrage in the market, you can still look closer to home. In fact, you can look *at* your home.

If you think about it, leveraging the equity in your home and looking for an arbitrage opportunity makes perfect sense, as long as it creates a cash flow and is relatively liquid. However, since this is your home we're talking about, you have to learn how to get over the emotional ties and attachments you have to it and look at it as purely a stepping-stone to creating further wealth. That is not to say that you should disregard everything and gamble away your equity. This is not Las Vegas; we're talking about your home here. But you *can* still safely deploy dollars that are imprisoned in your home into a situation that creates an arbitrage and builds your wealth without dealing with too much risk.

Why You Have to Change Your Thinking

As we've discussed in previous chapters, people are living longer and pension plans are going away. With the imminent threat of rising tax brackets, we can only expect that by retirement, many of us will be earning enough to be subject to them, especially if we are trying to preserve our lifestyles. I've never yet met a person who's said, "I really want to retire poor and I want to be restricted on what I can do, now that I have all the time on my hands that I need."

That just isn't anybody's goal, so think about what you want for yourself and what you'll face as you plan for retirement, and then consider using your mortgage as a means to an improved retirement picture.

It's natural to have some fear of risk, especially when it involves your home. Because of this fear, I think it is instructive to examine the root of it and how things have changed.

Where the Fear Comes From

The fear some people have for their mortgages is probably rooted in the Great Depression, when banks, desperate for cash, began issuing "mortgage calls," a practice that demanded borrowers pay all of their mortgages, sometimes in as little as thirty days.

Despite protective mechanisms in place to avoid a similar event and the passage of some seventy years, mortgage anxiety remains strong and seems to have been passed on from generation to generation as an insidious tradition. "My parents paid off their home in time for retirement, so I must do the same" is the thinking—never mind that you won't have enough money to live on in retirement and that you'll no longer have tax deductions to offset your retirement income, which is taxed as ordinary income. Does this really sound like a wise plan?

Anti-mortgage Homeowners

There are two kinds of people who are anti-mortgage: those who fear them, and those who believe that mortgages cost huge amounts of money in interest charges. We've already resolved the former issue, that fear thing, so let me dispel the folklore surrounding the interest question.

Carrying a mortgage is not harmful to your finances. Your home can gain or lose value regardless of what your mortgage situation is, and using the money that would go toward an early payoff for investments is much more profitable. If you value asset protection, you'll get the equity out of your home now and place it where it's not desirable for a creditor to access it. Also, if a natural disaster hits and destroys your home, you could be without that valuable equity for a long time, or even permanently. That equity only exists as long as the home is standing and even with insurance, you only have a *potential* right to coverage; also, it takes a long time to receive and may not pay what you thought your home was worth.

This group that focuses on the long-term costs feels that way because they know that over the life of a thirty-year loan, they will spend much more on interest than the purchase price of the house. In fact, when you look at that closing statement and what you'll have paid for the home in the next thirty years, it is sometimes shocking. But mortgage rates are still relatively low if you have good credit, and solid investments will return, over the thirty-year life of your mortgage, much more than the 6.5 to 8.5 percent they cost.

Even long-term government bonds pay nearly that amount. But giving your money to the bank to avoid a six- to eight-percent interest charge is denying yourself the opportunity to invest that money where it might earn eight to ten percent tax-deferred. In other words, the money you might have used to pay extra toward your mortgage could have been better used if it were put somewhere to grow using compound interest.

Home equity is not the same as cash in the bank; only cash is cash in the bank. Being house rich and cash poor is a dangerous position to be in. I have seen situations wherein it would have been far better to have access to the equity or value of a home and not to need it, than to need it and not be able to get at it. Keeping home equity safe is really a matter of positioning yourself to act instead of reacting to market conditions over which you have no control.

Housing prices can and do level off. They sometimes decline, as they currently have in Southern California, Arizona and Florida, where prices are taking significant corrective pushes downward. Real estate equity is no safer than any other investment with a value determined by an external market over which we personally have no control. In fact, due to the hidden risks of life, real estate equity is not nearly as safe as many other conservative investments and assets. Despite that fact, most Americans think that a home is *the* safest investment. In fact, for most Americans, a home is their largest investment, more than all of their other investments combined. I'm not a favor of diversification for its own sake, as I've said, but you do need to have diversification in the investments you choose for your portfolio. The question here is, Does holding large amounts of home equity put the homeowner at unnecessary risk? I think it does and have seen tragic situations wherein people were sued or their homes were consumed by natural disasters.

Rick Edelman, one of the top financial planners in the country and a *New York Times* best-selling author, summarizes this, in his book, *The Truth About Money*:

> Too often, people buy homes in a vacuum, without considering how that purchase is going to affect other aspects of their lives. This can be a big mistake, and therefore you must recognize that owning a home holds very important implications for the rest of your financial plan. Although a fine goal, owning a home is not the ultimate financial planning goal, and in fact how you handle issues of home ownership may well determine whether you achieve financial success.[70]

Robert Kiyosaki, in his book, *Rich Dad, Poor Dad*,[71] gives readers a complete paradigm shift on how money works and how they should view their homes. For example, rather than seeing an asset as something with value, as many see their homes, Robert's book defines an asset as something that generates cash flow. This means that according to Robert Kiyosaki's book, your home is not an asset.

---

[70] Rick Edelman, The Truth About Money, (NY: Harper Collins, 2004), 363.
[71] Kiyosaki.

I highly agree with this; it is the reason why I think it is prudent to examine whether or not you can create cash flow out of the imprisoned equity that sits in your home.

Home Equity Management (HEM)

Home equity loans are not something you should take lightly. Because they reduce the equity in your home, it requires a balancing act to do this right. But, if you do get it right, you'll have liquid investments that offer solid rates of return and take advantage of arbitrage opportunities.

I don't want you taking a home equity loan to buy that big-screen TV you've always wanted. This is about generating cash flow. Life insurance is the tool of choice because cash in the policy grows tax-free and can be accessed tax-free in retirement through policy loans.

If you are considering taking a home equity loan, know that the interest on the home equity may not be deductible. Title 26, Section 163 of the Internal Revenue Code[72] dictates that home equity debt (which includes a refinance with removal of equity) is only deductible up to $100,000 of new debt. Also, if you plan on earning cash from the investments made with the borrowed money, then the interest is not deductible.

Many people have read a book called *Missed Fortune 101* by Douglas Andrews. While the book details some of the opportunities available, it does not go into depth on how home equity is affected by IRC Section 264(a) 3, which eliminates the home mortgage interest deduction when equity is removed and repositioned into cash-value life insurance. There will be more information about the tax implications of equity harvesting at the end of this chapter.

Most advisors or consumers trying to do this type of planning have read the books or been to the sales seminars that emphasize how powerful this concept is as a sales tool (which is true). Life insurance agents use equity harvesting to sell large amounts of life insurance,

---

[72] Internal Revenue Code of the United States Code (26 U.S.C. 1986) http://www.law.cornell.edu/uscode/html/uscode26/usc_sup_01_26.html, [accessed January 2, 2008].

and mortgage brokers use it to sell mortgages, and so-called advisors are doing both. However, many consumers and advisors are missing a crucial fact that needs to be considered: whether or not the mortgage-interest deduction still applies. See the end of the chapter for a more in-depth look at this. Home equity management will work even if you do not take the interest deduction. I think it merits running the numbers but in most cases, you'll find that what you can achieve will be well worth any risk involved in putting your money to work for you.

For years, business owners have used their home equity to build their businesses. Some very famous entrepreneurs have done this to get ahead when they needed capital for quantum leaps in their enterprises. Why not consider yourself in the business of investing in your future by taking this non-performing asset and turning it into something that creates a return for you? You have to make sure you can afford the increased mortgage payments, but consider this a payment toward your retirement or investment portfolio, and don't gamble it. Place it in safe assets that guarantee a return without risk to your principal.

The habit people have of pouring everything into their mortgages shows a lack of understanding of liquidity considerations, and it seems that misinformed debtors with risk-aversion prefer paying off debt obligations early, thereby losing the opportunity for wealth accumulation through arbitrage.

Recently, the NASD issued an alert because, they said, "…we are concerned that investors who must rely on investment returns to make their mortgage payments could end up defaulting on their home loans if their investments decline and they are unable to meet their monthly mortgage payments." The NASD is on-target in advising against separating equity if you must rely on the returns from your investments to make the mortgage payments. Using home equity for wealth creation won't work if you're already against the wall in making your mortgage payments. You need to get your finances in order before you consider doing this.

Using home equity to increase your wealth without the mortgage-interest deduction is still reasonable while residential lending rates are at historic lows. You need to really run the numbers before trying this strategy. And remember, not all insurance policies are created equal, if that is where your harvested equity dollars will be deployed. This can work wonders, but there isn't a lot of room for error, so make sure it is done correctly.

If you're considering home equity management, you need to be aware of some of the possible scams and pitfalls out there. Too many people have fallen victim to scams and theft when dealing with home equity, and the FTC has provided the following warnings:

- Do not agree to a home equity loan if you don't have enough income to make the monthly payments.
- Do not sign any document you haven't read or any document that has blank spaces to be filled in after you sign.
- Do not let anyone pressure you into signing any document.
- Do not agree to a loan that includes credit insurance or extra products you don't want.
- Don't let the promise of extra cash or lower monthly payments get in the way of your good judgment about whether the cost you will ultimately pay for the loan is really worth it.
- Do not deed your property to anyone. First consult an attorney, a knowledgeable family member or someone else you trust.[73]

The most important reason why you don't want to give the bank any more money than is necessary is that cash is king. Having a home fully paid for is one thing, but being able to cover that unexpected medical expense is another. You'll need cash to pay for a family member's wedding, start a business or to send a kid to college, or just to use until you can recoup your insurance payout if a natural disaster hits your area.

If you were to suddenly experience difficult financial times, would you rather have $25,000 in cash to help you make your mortgage

---

[73] Federal Trade Commission, "Home Equity Loans: Borrowers Beware!" Federal Trade Commission, April 1998, http://www.ftc.gov/bcp/edu/pubs/consumer/homes/rea11.shtm [accessed January 2, 2008].

payment, or an additional $25,000 in equity trapped in your home? Most people who attempt to file bankruptcy could have avoided it with only $10,000 cash saved for that moment of emergency in their lives. Almost every person who has ever lost his or her home to foreclosure would be better off if the equity had been separated from the home in a liquid, safe, conservative side fund that could be used to make mortgage payments during a time of need.

Now, let's take a look at an example and use some real-world numbers. John is a homeowner who bought a home for $693,000 and put down $138,600 in order to conform to the required twenty percent for an option arm loan. John intends to make the minimum monthly payment of $2,129.56, and will put away $750 per month in a life insurance policy, using the money that would ordinarily be used to pay a thirty-year fixed rate mortgage, which would have been around $4,380 if at a 6.5 percent interest rate. John's minimum payments will increase each year by 7.5 percent from the previous year's payment, so next year's will be $2,289.27.

If John uses the technique of making two payments per month on the minimum payment (e.g., $1,144.63 times 2), he will create a slight equity build that slows down his deferral and stays on track with the build-up in his policy. This will capture a triple compound over time, since it builds up tax-free. ("Triple compound" means earning interest on the principal, earning interest on the taxes you would have had to pay, and earning interest on the interest that builds in your investment).

After two years and two months, John's outstanding deferred interest is $24,107.45 with a full interest rate of 7.690 percent. The build-up in his policy is $22,115.78. After examining the policy, I found out that $19.97 per month was being spent on an unnecessary rider that could be cut to create better performance.

The difference between the outstanding deferral and what is created in the policy after insurance costs is $1,991.67 and not a significant enough difference to deter John from doing equity management, which could create a tax-free income for life of $80,000 per year. The key to this type of planning is a trained professional who not only knows how to structure the loan properly to mitigate rapid deferral, but also knows the right insurance products and does not oversell riders and unnecessary components of the policy. At the time of this writing, there is one carrier who credits 140 percent of the S&P, which will create phenomenal results as we head into a less-robust market.

Another good question to ask yourself is, "How long do I intend to live in the home?" This strategy is ideal for those who know that this will not be their residence for life, but may just be a temporary stage. Nonetheless, even if it is a residence for life, it may be worth earning interest on the equity that otherwise sits there earning zero cash flow, and could be lost due to a market fluctuation, lawsuit or natural disaster.

I think everyone who expects to retire on time and live a full life, which could be thirty to forty years in retirement, will need to seriously consider equity management and the possibility of repositioning it into liquid assets that create a compound return. Finding the right people to assist will be crucial, since there are an excess of advisors out there—mostly incompetent when it comes to running the numbers and understanding your situation in light of the tax implications.

Some Information About the Tax Implications of Home Equity Management

When you get into managing your home equity, you need to understand that there are tax implications that limit what you can deduct on your taxes. IRC section 264 regulates the available deductions and stipulates that several items, including single premium life insurance, annuity contracts and personal interest (this means anything other than items such as investment interest, trade or business interest, etc) are not deductible.

Make sure you consult a tax attorney when you're considering deducting interest on a home equity loan. You need to make sure you qualify for the deduction. There are other regulations that come in to play, like the plan-of-purchase rule, so make sure you've done your research before investing your home equity dollars.

Does Section 264(a) Destroy Arbitrage Associated With HEM?

Are you kidding? No! In fact, it may make the most sense to give you a quantum leap in your investing. There are ways to plan so that the interest on home equity debt (refinanced debt with cash removal) is deductible under 264(a). For instance, a person could refinance and take out money to pay down other debt that would free up money paid on those debts, and then could use this new freed-up money to make payments on the insurance premiums or design the plan using the four-out-of-seven rule discussed above.

What We Learned

1. You get no tax break when giving the bank principal. You save on taxes only when you pay interest.

2. Money you invest is taxed at a lower rate than your savings would amount to from tax-deductible interest. Therefore, you want to maximize your interest payment while minimizing your principal payment.

3. Money you give to the bank is money you'll never see again.

4. You don't earn any interest on your equity and when you need cash from it, it might not be available to you. If you ever suffer a job loss, major medical, home destruction (as happened in Hurricane Katrina) or other financial crisis, you could find yourself unable to get a home loan.

5. The best way to achieve a free and clear title, if you really want it, is by mortgaging your home to the utmost. Increasing the loan, investing the equity and then accumulating enough to pay off the debt is possibly the quickest method to eliminating a mortgage. Modest assumptions show it to be much faster than a fifteen-year mortgage that sends more money to the bank.

6. Mortgages don't lower home values. Your house will grow in value (or not) whether or not you have a mortgage.

7. Your mortgage is the cheapest money you'll ever buy. Most people need to borrow money during their lives, so why pay eighteen percent to credit cards when you can borrow at rates of seven percent or less? Using this money for investments, not speculation like the stock market, will allow you to arbitrage these dollars.

CHAPTER SEVENTEEN

Creating Your Financial Blueprint

We discussed estate planning briefly, in Chapter Twelve, as a part of the process of securing what you've earned through investments. If you recall, securing what you've earned is the fourth of five steps inside of the Three Secret Pillars of Wealth.

As I always preach to people in my seminars, wealth building, and the securing of that wealth, takes having a solid blueprint. You wouldn't trust a builder to put your home together if he didn't have blueprints, so why are you winging it when it comes to securing the dollars you've worked so hard to earn?

Estate planning is massively important to anyone with assets. Your passing will be hard enough for your relatives and business partners; don't make it even more difficult by exposing your estate to lawsuits, probate fees and other costs. In this chapter, we're going to look at some terms you need to understand before planning your estate and some of the risks you face as a business or property owner. All of the topics we'll be looking at are important to understand if you want to truly protect yourself and your loved ones.

I've created a quadrant that breaks down four key areas of estate planning for any size estate, from one worth a few hundred thousand to one worth billions.

BURNS ESTATE PLANNING QUADRANT

BASE PLAN	ESTATE FREEZE
RISK MANAGEMENT AKA ASSET PROTECTION	ESTATE DRAIN

In the upper left-hand corner, you have the base plan; in the lower left-hand corner

You have the risk management plan, or in sexier terms, "asset protection." In the upper right-hand corner is the estate freeze plan and in the lower right-hand corner, you have estate-draining techniques. I am going to briefly go over some of this, but this book is not intended to be an extensive treatise on estate planning, as we could go on for chapters on each area. But I do want you to be aware of the big picture and the importance of at least having the base plan, since it is appropriate for just about everyone who is not in poverty.

Base Plan

The base plan has three layers, with the top layer being what I refer to as the "departure documents." There are three departure documents, including the revocable living trust, the pourover will and the general assignment.

Revocable Living Trust

A trust is really an agreement between you and someone you've assigned to manage your assets. Therefore, a revocable trust, sometimes called a "living trust," is really just an agreement you can revoke or amend during your lifetime. In fact, you can even act as the trustee of your trust while you're first starting out, and then move the assets to a company that has more experience.

When you die, the terms of your trust become irrevocable and your assets are allocated accordingly. The terms of the trust become irrevocable upon the trustor's death. Because the trust contains provisions that provide for the distribution of your assets on and after your death, the trust acts as a substitute for your will, and eliminates the need for the probate of your will with respect to those assets that were held in your living trust at your death.

Trusts can be designed in many different ways, depending on what the size of the estate's worth is and what the estate tax credit is at the time of creating the living trust. At the time of this printing, the individual estate tax credit is $2,000,000 per person or $4,000,000 for a married couple who preserves their credits with a trust.

Will

A will simply names the people who will receive your assets upon your death. When crafting a will, you'll need to nominate an executor, who will manage and distribute your estate in addition to paying debts and settling accounts. In your will, you will also name the guardians for your children should they be underage upon your death. Remember, only assets in your name will be subject to your will.

Pourover Will

Pourover wills are used as catch-alls, to ensure that all of your assets will flow into your trust in case you didn't have time to retitle them in the name of the trust prior to your death. A pourover will acts as an addition to your already existing will or trust.

General Assignment

A general assignment of personal property takes care of property that doesn't have a title to it. This includes things like tools, sporting equipment, etc. Make sure that you're specific about what goes to whom upon your death. If you have jewelry and other miscellaneous items of value, a general assignment will be helpful to your executor in knowing who gets all of the untitled property you own.

The Second Layer

The second layer of the base plan is designed to deal with incapacity issues. These deal with people who are still alive but have been rendered incapable of making decisions on their own, due to traumatic injury, stroke or any other frailty that could arise.

Durable Power of Attorney

A "durable" POA is one that remains in force even after you lose mental capacity. Some people don't realize that power of attorney is really only good until you become incapacitated. You need to make sure that your power of attorney is "durable" so that your family, or whomever you've granted this power to, doesn't have to go to court to secure it.

Healthcare Directives

These documents, or their absence, have made news in recent years as high-profile cases have seen families battling over the healthcare decisions of loved ones. Having a healthcare directive ensures that someone, whom you've chosen, will have the power to decide whether to accept or decline health measures on your behalf, should you become incapacitated. The "agent" assigned by you (usually an attorney) must act according to your wishes. This document also provides you with some legal protections because the agent can be removed from the decision-making process should he or she act illegally or contrary to your written wishes.

Without one of these documents, lengthy legal battles can arise in the case of medical incapacitation, as happened in the case of Terry Schiavo, who lingered for years in a vegetative state while her family fought it out in the courts, trying to decide what she would have wanted.

When I counsel clients who are domestic partners or who are going in on real estate together, I always recommend that they get these documents done to give non-family members the authority to act on their behalf. Imagine what would happen if you had a partner in real property who went into a seizure one day and never recovered. Without having the durable power of attorney, you would have no authority to get things done with the property, including selling it without the person's signature. Transactions would literally be frozen.

Other
The final layer of the base plan can include community property agreements, separate property agreements, deeds for retitling real property, and over 160 strategies to accomplish the other corners of the quadrant.

Over the last seven years, I've focused on assisting real estate investors with both tax efficiency and risk management, and I think the easiest way to learn some of the lessons I've learned is by example. Therefore, I'm going to go over one particular case that recently came into my office, wherein all the work the investor did could have been undone in any one of several ordinary events.

Investor Joe
(Names have been changed to protect the uninformed.)

When Joe came into my office, he was sixty-two years old, divorced with adult children, and had just purchased ten properties, nine of them all around the country. He had overbought in two areas, in my opinion, which violated the basic theory of diversification—but more on that later.

Joe held titles on some of the properties with his daughter, and some with his ex-spouse. According to him, neither of them was stable in their personal finances. He had no estate plan, no incapacity plan, no life insurance and no umbrella insurance. How many issues can my savvy investors see right away?

Remember the facts:

- Sixty-two years old

- On title with daughter
- On title with ex-spouse
- No living trust
- No durable power of attorney
- No limited liability entity

Potential Issues:

Q: At this age, is he vulnerable to death, incapacity or severe illness?
A: Yes, of course he is.

Q: Was the jointly held property with his daughter a gift, possibly exceeding his annual exclusion?
A: This is an open question, but it appears to be a gift, absent a document to the contrary, like some type of note.

Q: Was the jointly held property with the ex-spouse a gift?
A: Same as above—this is his ex-spouse, so no special treatment.

Q: If Joe had a stroke or other incapacitation, would his daughter have the authority to act on his behalf?
A: No. She may need to go to court and get a court appointment. This may be required in each and every state where they own property together.

Q: If Joe had a stroke or other incapacitation, would his ex-spouse have the authority to act on his behalf?
A: Same as above.

Q: If Joe died and his ex-spouse could not qualify for the loan on a property, would she lose a step-up in basis creating capital gains when she sold it?
A: Yes. The ex-spouse lost this by being on title. The better transfer would have been through Joe's living trust.

Q: If Joe died and his daughter could not qualify for the loan on a property, when she sold it, would she lose a step-up in basis creating capital gains?
A: Yes, same as above.

Q: When any of the jointly held properties are sold, does Joe kill half of the step up in basis creating capital gains tax?
A: Yes. One-half of the property will not be subject to capital gains tax upon the sale, since the step-up in basis is lost. Also, if the other parties keep the properties, they are required to submit a death certificate, and this could create reassessment.

Q: If Joe were sued due to an event on one of the properties that exceeded his ordinary hazard insurance, would his personal assets be at risk?
A: Yes. If he didn't have enough insurance, then the titleholder of the property would be responsible, which means that everything he owns is up for grabs.

Q: If Joe died, would his estate have nine probates to take care of in other states before they could bring them back to California, where he was a resident?
A: Yes. Without a doubt, and this would be expensive.

Q: Can Joe pass his properties, which have appreciated over the years, to his descendents at a discount?
A: No. This can only be done by using either an LLC or family limited partnership (FLP).

Q: Does Joe have a way of removing his personal assets from a lawsuit connected to liability on a property?
A: No. All his assets are exposed.

Q: Did Joe limit the remedy a complainant can get from him because of an injury on the property?
A: No. You can only limit a creditor to a charging order remedy with an LLC or FLP.

Just as a quick mention, Joe did not have any life insurance, which means that someone would have to find liquid dollars to pay his portion of the loan, or the entire loan on each property. A loan is only based upon the income of the individual who applied and does not automatically transfer to the joint titleholder. This could mean a mass liquidation of properties at perhaps a bad time in the market, creating terrible losses.

Also, Joe didn't have any long-term care, which in my mind is another form of asset protection planning, since it prevents confiscation of assets by the government if you need state nursing home assistance.

As you can see, it was great that Joe tried to be wealthy, but he didn't think like an investor and instead created ten catastrophic situations in one buying spree. To think like an investor, you have to know that when building, just as a contractor builds a house, you need your blueprint to stay on course. Contractors don't go and just take the tools and materials and go for it. They follow detailed blueprints that are designed to create well-structured homes.

Similarly, when you build wealth, you need your blueprint before you start buying anything. You need your wealth vision, and this starts with having a unified plan on paper, and all the documents that support that plan.

Joint Tenancy As an Anti-probate Strategy

Unmarried individuals holding property as joint tenants may have to pay double estate taxes. The results for married couples can be equally costly because the surviving spouse would not get the full benefit of the step up in tax basis upon the other spouse's death. In other words, the surviving spouse, in selling a property held as community property instead of joint tenants, could save significant taxes on the resale of the property.

Recent case law also allows couples to save significant estate taxes on community property by allowing them to take a fifteen-percent valuation discount. Usually, the benefit of the added creditor protection for joint tenancy property is far less than the benefits of holding property as community property.

Also, if you are on title with your sons or daughters, and they have creditors, those creditors are going to come for half of your home. Joint tenancy is not a well-groomed planning strategy.

Asset Protection

Over 80 million lawsuits are filed each year in the US. Each year, trial attorneys create new causes of action aimed at the perceived deep pockets of businesses and individuals.

For instance, most people are familiar with the infamous McDonald's hot coffee case and lately, the mold cases. *The San Francisco Chronicle* reported on January 22, 2003, that tenants of an apartment building in Hayward were suing the owner for $5 million for mold-related injuries. Mold damage awards in recent cases have been so great that the major property insurance companies are reluctant to write policies in California. It may be a limitation or exclusion in your policy.

Not so long ago, you did not get sued unless you did something wrong. Today, this is not the case. The prevailing philosophy is, if something bad happens, someone else must pay, and many people are willing to take their chances with the twelve-person lottery—the jury—to try to win big.

The "someone else must pay" attitude is encouraged by our contingency-fee legal system. The litigation playing field is not level. Plaintiff attorneys take contingency fees, resulting in plaintiffs getting free lawyers. The English rule of "loser pays" doesn't apply to personal injury cases in the US. Once a suit is filed, you've lost. You have to pay an attorney to defend the suit, and even if your insurance company pays for the defense (and don't count on that), you must spend time and emotional energy as the defendant.

Firm planning can drastically reduce your risk of being a defendant in a lawsuit. Understanding the risks of property ownership will help you see that planning is crucial for your protection.

Owning rental property in your name is not wise. Any lawsuit related to the property will be directed at the owner. Two types of risks can affect rental property: inside risks and outside risks. Inside risks include those related to the property, such as injuries to tenants and their guests, and damages to tenants' property. Outside risks are unrelated to the property, such as a car accident, a business transaction, a business injury or a malpractice claim. If you are sued for a risk unrelated to the property, all of your personal assets will be exposed, including all property owned in your name.

Joint Ownership

Many people own property with a relative or friend. This form of ownership is called "tenancy in common." Each owner owns an undivided share of the property. Joint ownership with a right of survivorship is similar, except that when one of the owners dies, the surviving owner gets the deceased owner's share.

Both forms of joint ownership create much more liability than if you owned the property in your name alone. If one owner is at risk for lawsuits and claims for outside risks, then multiple owners multiply the risk. If you and your friend own a property and he is sued and loses, the plaintiff could get your friend's share of the property and become your new partner. With joint ownership, your co-owner's risks become your risks.

Community Property

In California, assets acquired during marriage are considered community property—each spouse owns one half. While this is often a fair division of assets, it presents problems. Property owned as community property is subject to the creditors of either spouse. If the husband is sued and loses, the wife's share of the community property may be fair game for the plaintiff, unless the property is formally separated in writing and there is a proper exchange for value.

If you own several properties dispersed amongst several states, you could be facing multiple probates. What is the significance of this? In California, if you don't have a living trust or other estate-planning tool, and your gross estate is valued over $100,000, your heirs will have to go to court to have your assets distributed. This is a loss in time and can be expensive.

The California fees are set by statute and start out at four percent on the first $15,000, three percent on the next $85,000, two percent on the next $900,000, and it continues, but you get the picture. Thus, the probate fee on a $100,000 estate is $3,150, the fee on a $500,000 estate would be $11,150 and the fee on a $1 million estate would be $21,150—coupled with the attorney's extraordinary fees (for traveling to court, etc.) and the court's fees.

In addition to the probate and state fees, there are basic burial or funeral expenses, administrative fees, payment of debts and possible death taxes. When you combine the probate and court fees of several different states, you have a significant reduction in your estate that is unnecessary and was avoidable for a fraction of the price, by implementing an estate plan that avoids probate.

Here are a few simple steps you can take to provide better protection of your real estate investments.

Step One: Carry Proper Insurance

A good insurance policy can provide a solid first line of defense. However, you must be aware of its limitations.

General business insurance policies insure against accidents on the business property, such as slip-and-falls, fire and equipment malfunction. These policies often exclude accidents occurring outside the scope of employment, an intentional act by an owner or employee, contract claims and work done at home.

Liability policies for professionals, such as doctors, dentists, attorneys, architects, engineers and accountants, also have exclusions from coverage, such as grossly negligent acts, willful or wanton misconduct, punitive damages and liability related to product liability.

Personal liability insurance policies include auto, homeowner's and umbrella coverage. If a plaintiff's damages exceed your auto policy limits, you will be personally liable for the balance. Homeowner's insurance policies provide insurance for damage to the residence caused by acts of God, insects and often, construction defects. The policies often exclude coverage for any business activities at the home.

Umbrella insurance policies are a relatively inexpensive way to supplement auto and homeowner's policy limits, but they are not complete. Umbrella policies generally exclude coverage for dangerous sports, dangerous equipment, such as guns, trampolines, swimming pools, and sometimes lawn mowers, chain saws and power tools. In addition, such policies may exclude dog bites, intentional acts and business activities.

Another problem with relying exclusively on insurance is the risk that your insurance company may not be in business when you file a claim. *The Wall Street Journal* reported on January 30, 2003[74] that a rash of insolvencies among insurers resulted in hundreds of thousands of consumers at risk of not collecting on their claims. The problem is growing as more and more insurance companies are filing for bankruptcy. While insurance is a good first step, it not always reliable.

Step Two: Title Properties in a Limited Liability Entity

The best way to own rental property is in a limited liability entity (LLE), such as a limited partnership (LP) or limited liability company (LLC). Instead of owning property in your name or with a partner, you can establish an LLC and transfer title of the property to the LLC. The LLC now owns the property and you and/or your members own the LLC. This common transaction will provide substantial benefits.

Protection From Inside Risks

When an LLC owns property, your personal exposure for inside risks is limited to your investment in the LLC. If a tenant sues, he can't get to your personal assets, such as your house and bank accounts, absent extraordinary facts. The LLC statutes limit his recovery to

---

[74] Christopher Oster, "Troubled insurers halt payments," Wall Street Journal, January 30, 2003,

your investment in the LLC in general, unless there is fraud involved. By owning your property in an LLC, you will limit your exposure to inside risk and protect your other assets.

Protection From Outside Risks

If you lose a lawsuit, the plaintiff receives a judgment against you and becomes your judgment creditor. The judgment creditor cannot reach the LLC property because it is protected by statute. In most cases, all a judgment creditor can get from the LLC is a charging order. A charging order does not give him control or management rights over the LLC, nor does it allow him to reach the LLC property. A charging order only gives the judgment creditor a right to receive your share of LLC profits, if any.

If the LLC has a net income after expenses, you and your LLC members must elect whether to distribute the income to yourselves or use the income for capital improvements to the property. If the LLC makes no distributions to its owners, the judgment creditor gets nothing.

If a charging order has been levied against your LLC interest, it may be in your best interest to elect against distributions. You won't get income, but neither will the judgment creditor. In fact, he may even have to pay your share of LLC income taxes.

An LLC is a pass-through entity. It does not pay taxes; its owners do. If the LLC has net income, whether it is distributed or not, its owners must pay income taxes on their proportionate shares. Here are two examples to clarify the point:

> *Example 1*: Protectem, LLC has three equal members. The LLC net income is $60,000, which is distributed equally to each member. Each member is then responsible for taxes on $20,000, which will be reported on their individual 1040 returns.

> *Example 2*: Protectem, LLC nets $60,000, but reinvests the income into property improvements. The members don't

receive distributions, but each will still be responsible for the tax on their share of the LLC income, which is $20,000. There may even be a capital call requiring each member to place more capital into the entity.

If the LLC has net income, the owners pay tax whether or not they actually receive their shares of the income. The holder of a charging order has a right to profits; therefore, the IRS may consider him responsible for the taxes, not you. This concept will likely turn a charging order into a poison pill for the judgment creditor.

Example 3: A judgment creditor has a charging order against John, a partner in Protectem, LLC. Protectem has a net income of $60,000, which the partners decide to reinvest in improvements to the properties. The judgment creditor is responsible for taxes on John's $20,000, even though they received no distribution of income.

A judgment creditor with a charging order has a right to your share of the LLE profits. However, even if he receives no distributions, he may be saddled with your share of the taxes.

With no right to reach or sell the LLC property, no LLC management or control rights, no guarantee of LLC income, and a potential tax liability, a charging order is not a desirable asset. If a plaintiff understands the diminished returns of a charging order, he may think twice about bringing the lawsuit. If a plaintiff goes forward and wins, he may likely be willing to settle for a reduced amount, rather than face potential tax liability on income he may never receive.

A properly drafted LLC is not a foolproof protection against lawsuits, but it will better protect your income property and your personal assets. It will also significantly improve your position against a plaintiff and judgment creditor. Pre-planning is the only planning that works. If you wait until you are sued, it will be too late. Once a claim or suit is filed against you, your property is exposed. Plan now and protect the many benefits of owning rental property.

There are other strategies that are better left to real time and should not be discussed outside of attorney/client privilege, in my opinion, so this is not a replete list of what to do or what can be done.

Financial

In follow-up to the Fortuna Triangle that was introduced in Chapter Five, I use the Burns Financial Quadrant to be sure we take a holistic approach and treat the entire needs of a client's finances. In the quadrant, you'll note that unlike many planning circles, we do not forget about real estate.

In the numerous financials I've reviewed for clients, I've seen that in many cases, their home and their investment properties made up the bulk of their worth. To ignore real estate in financial planning is to do a disservice to the client. In the bottom left-hand corner of the quadrant, we examine all manner of retirement plans, from traditional to self-directed plans, which I think are much better than traditional.

In the upper right-hand corner, I deal with cash flows, which usually involve taking a look at non-qualified planning or using properly structured life insurance to create tax-free income for life.

In the bottom right-hand corner of the quadrant, I have money management. I think of money management as being for people with $2 million in liquid assets that are ready to bear the burden of management fees.

Estate Drain
Gifting

Obviously, one of the more common ways of avoiding leaving a large estate, subject to taxes, to your beneficiaries is to simply give it away while you're still alive. Now, giving away some of your income or property doesn't exclude you from income taxes and gift taxes, if the amount is large enough. Everyone currently has a lifetime gift exemption of $2 million and is allowed up to $12,000 a year to give away without reporting it to the IRS, but future changes could affect this either negatively or positively.

It makes sense to give away assets early because any growth could put them into a new taxable category, and any growth will benefit the person you've given the gift to. Once you've exhausted your lifetime gift allowance and you make gifts of more than the annual gift exclusion, you'll have to pay gift taxes on anything you give away or sell for less than its value. Even with the gift taxes, you might still be better off giving away your assets and avoiding the estate tax, which currently runs higher than the gift tax rate.

Again, this plays into the "tax the seed" mentality I have. If you give your assets to your beneficiary now, then you'll be taxed only on the initial offering. If you wait years, or until your death, to give away the assets, you'll be taxed on a much larger amount, taking money out of the hands of the beneficiary.

Another good way to give a gift is to pay for someone's tuition or medical costs. You just need to make sure you pay the institution directly.

Family Limited Partnership or Limited Liability Company

A family limited partnership (FLP) or a limited liability company (LLC) can provide important tax and non-tax benefits. From a non-tax standpoint, these entities are important in that they can provide vehicles for managing family assets, and can protect you from liabilities arising in connection with the assets held in the FLP or LLC. They can also provide asset protection in that a creditor who wins an interest from you will succeed only concerning your rights in the entity, and may not be able to force a liquidation of the partnership.

From a gift and estate tax planning standpoint, an FLP or LLC can give rise to significant valuation discounts, which effectively drain the estate by coupling the gifting of partnership or membership interests to your loved ones.

Some of the other techniques fall into the estate freeze, and this can get really complex, so my recommendation is to hire a really good estate-planning lawyer to help you through these issues. I'll try to explain a little bit about the process to help you understand it before you speak to an attorney.

Estate Freeze

These techniques freeze the value of your assets at today's prices, for transfer to a trust for gift and estate tax purposes, so that the future appreciation will transfer to the benefit of the remaining beneficiaries outside your estate. You would also discount the value of the gift for gift tax purposes.

While I don't want to bore you with every method for estate freeze, I do have one technique that I want to discuss, since it is the one that a large amount of the population can use, especially in regions of the country where real property has appreciated significantly over the years.

Qualified Personal Residence Trust (QPRT)

The idea behind this trust is to provide you with a way of gifting your personal residence to a beneficiary while avoiding some of the gift taxes and estate taxes associated with such a transfer. Essentially, you transfer ownership of your home to the trust and remain living there until a set time, when ownership will transfer to the beneficiary.

The whole purpose here is to get a highly appreciated home out of the estate to reduce the potential of estate taxes. I have had clients with $2.5 million homes who paid $50,000 for them, creating an appreciated asset of $2,450,000, which is significant and worthy of an examination of this technique. Keep in mind that a residence donated to the QPRT cannot be reacquired by the donor by buying it back from the QPRT.

In addition to the methods of preserving your estate that we've discussed, you may also want to consider charitable strategies in your planning. There are various charitable strategies that create further opportunities not only to contribute to society but also to transfer and protect large amounts of wealth. It's worth looking into.

What We Learned

1. Everyone needs to evaluate estate planning or incapacity planning.

2. If you own multiple properties in several states, you need a way to bring them all together to avoid multiple probates.

3. There are two steps for protective planning you can take today: 1) Carry property insurance and 2) title in the name of a limited liability entity.

4. It may be appropriate to use a limited liability entity to hold your investment properties for protection, tax purposes and estate-planning purposes.

5. Estate planning has four quadrants that deal with a base plan, risk management, estate drain and estate freeze.

CHAPTER EIGHTEEN

Putting It All Together: "Plodding wins the race."[75]

Success is not always about what you have today; instead, it's about what you've put in place today that sets in motion your successes of tomorrow. This chapter is dedicated to showing you the need for long-term planning and how things work when what we've learned is put together.

I have clients who have been hugely successful, or are on the path to success, and every one of them understands the need to stay on a planned path for success. It is like taking the tortoise's approach to investing over the hare's approach, *a la* Aesop's fable, and I think you'll find that it's the best way to secure your future.

Robert Kiyosaki's book, *Prophecy*, he predicted grave financial consequences for the unprepared. Kiyosaki criticized ERISA—the Employee Retirement Income Security Act, which provides regulations related to benefit and retirement plans—as having flaws that would manifest themselves in the years to come.[76] Now, the storm clouds have gathered and some twenty years after ERISA was signed into law, Kiyosaki's prophecy has begun to come true because of the misdeeds of corporate leaders.

On April 3, 2000, the US NASDAQ exchange recorded its biggest-ever one-day fall. Then, Enron and WorldCom filed two of the largest corporate bankruptcies in US history, wiping out thousands of jobs and their employees' hopes. With companies in

---

[75] Aesop, "The Tortoise and Hare," Aesop's Fables.300 BCE.
[76] Robert Kiyosaki and Sharon L. Lechter, "Rich Dad's Prophecy," (New York, Business Plus October, 9 2002) 24.

disarray and an ever-volatile stock market, Robert Kiyosaki says that the worst is still to come, and I totally agree with him.

Here is what we know about the retirement picture for many Americans: According to a survey performed by Lincoln Financial in 2004, prior to reaching retirement, fifty-four percent of current retirees had never thought about how many years they would spend in retirement, and forty-three percent had underestimated the amount of time they would spend in retirement.[77]

Because you can live twenty or thirty years beyond your retirement date, investment needs are growing and there is very little room for mistakes or non-performance. The average life spans for men and women are increasing, and chances are, you'll be alive long after retirement, which means careful planning is needed.

Reports show that numerous retirees go on spending sprees as soon as they retire, and some experts have provided credible statistics that show that many retirees have trouble managing their wealth, suggesting that they may be unable to support themselves in their later years. While more than half of new retirees saw their total wealth grow significantly between 1992 and 2001, some lost fifteen or more of their savings and twenty-one percent depleted at least a quarter of it, according to a study by the Employee Benefit Research Institute.[78]

The study showed that Hispanics, single women, divorcees and low-income workers without supplemental retirement income plans diminished their retirement wealth. White men, married couples and well-educated people fared better, especially where they had supplementary retirement income plans in place. The study included people born between 1931 and 1941, who were likely to have been the most financially disciplined since they are considered "post-Depression survivors." The average total wealth grew from $235,514 to $435,072 over the study's time period.

I want you to avoid the pitfalls that some of people in the study fell into, and you can do so by combining what you've learned in this

---

[77] Mathew Greenwald & Associates, "Lincoln Long Life Survey 2005," Lincoln Retirement Institute, http://www.lfg.com/LincolnPageServer?LFGPage=/lfg/lfgclient/rna/index.html&LFGContentID=/lfg/lfgclient/rna/surv, [January 28, 2008].

[78] "How to Increase Worker Savings? 401(k)s Provide Ideas," Employee Benefit Research Institute Retirement Confidence Survey 2005, p. 2.

book with what you teach yourself through experience and the advice of a professional planner.

It's important that you invest using the three pillars of wealth that you've learned about in this book. Make sure that your investments, whatever you decide to make them, take advantage of the power of leverage, arbitrage and cash flow, and provide you with the returns you demand—not the returns some anonymous money manager earns for you in the market.

As you retire on your lump-sum 401(k) distributions and other vehicles (e.g., an IRA), you'll find that you can benefit by having access to managed withdrawals or annuity payments that offer a more disciplined approach.[79]

To retire in Orange County, California, where my office is located, with $10,000 disposable income per month retirement income, a person would need to have saved $3,464,852.[80] The question you need to ask yourself is, Do you currently have a plan to save that much money by the time you retire? Today's sixty-five-year-olds are a mix of fifty-four percent dependent, thirty-six percent working, five percent dead, four percent financially independent ($3,000 per month of retirement income), and one percent wealthy.[81] Why, in the wealthiest country in the world, is only one percent of the population achieving wealth?

The answers are not clear, but we know that we like to enjoy our money, that we lack control and that our banking system, which is designed to promote credit cards, makes it easy to get trapped in debt. Don't fall victim to these temptations. Take what you've learned in this book and build a cohesive plan that uses all three pillars of wealth.

In addition to a lack of financial education among future retirees, there is another looming threat that will affect your prospects for a healthy and financially stable retirement. Long-term

---

[79] Arun Misra, "Many Retirees Deplete Wealth Too Quickly" Employee Benefit Adviser E-Newsletter, February 1, 2005, 47.
[80] This is using 2005 dollars and 3.49 percent inflation.
[81] "A Statistical Profile of Americans Aged 65+," Dept. of Health & Human Services, Administration on Aging, November 2006, http://www.aoa.gov/press/fact/pdf/ss_stat_profile.pdf [accessed January 30, 2008].

care costs are threatening to bankrupt Medicaid and the states that pay for it. The best hope for a cure lies in cutting down on the need for institutional care. With the population aging, states are struggling to balance the relentless need for nursing home care, increased demands for services and a way to fund it all. The Medicaid population is in need of expensive, long-term care services with even younger disabled adults unable to live independently without assistance.

What all of this means for you is that future assistance from the government is not guaranteed, and that the more retirement income you can provide for yourself and your family, the better off you'll be. Don't rely on a broken Medicaid program to help you pay for quality medical coverage. Plan now for your needs and think about what you'll require for a quality retirement.

What to Look Out For

When you drill down deep into the factors that lead to the creation of wealth and the factors that hinder it, you'll find that there are five destroyers of wealth. I created a mnemonic to help you remember them: TIPED, which stands for 1) Taxes 2) Inflation 3) Procrastination 4) Expenses and 5) Debt. If you can eliminate all or most of these, you can get ahead.

But, it will require determination and commitment on your part. Nothing great happens until you commit and match your desire to live your dreams by taking action. This is going to take your being very involved in your life, and a serious look at your finances. You'll need to act like a responsible financial officer of your own enterprise. If not, your financial future might be bleak, and it's unlikely the government will be there to bail you out.

The New Millionaire

According to Belinda Goldsmith of Reuters, a new research study performed by private wealth specialists Lewis Schiff and Russ Alan Prince found that "more and more Americans worth at least $1 million want luxury goods but otherwise lead family-focused, work-oriented lives." According to Goldsmith, "The same study found that the number of Americans with $1 million to $10 million had risen to more than eight million households."[82] That's 7.6 percent of US households—a number that is growing at fifteen percent a year. Are you going to be a part of this amazing growth? What would happen if you made some modifications to your financial lifestyle and stuck to them? Could you be among these emerging middle-millionaires? The answer is "yes"—you can choose to create an incredible outcome because putting things in motion today creates incredible results tomorrow. Even if you never make it among the middle-millionaires during your working days, you can be among them when you retire.

Case Scenario

As an example to get you started, let's look at two fictional clients named Jack and Kate, and examine what the results of their twenty-year paths look like. Here are their facts: Jack is a professional and Kate works part-time. Together, they make about $150,000 per year. If that seems high, remember that Jack and Kate live in California, where the median income for a home of three is $150,000. So, as a baseline, Jack and Kate are pretty ordinary.

Jack has a 401(k) or pension plan with an accumulated value of $800,000. He didn't fully maximize his contributions, though, because he recognized that being taxed on the harvest would be worse than the seed. So, Jack retained some after-tax dollars to put away as supplemental retirement income.

In a properly structured life insurance policy, Jack overfunded and put more into cash values than the cost of the life insurance, so that it would build tax-free and provide tax-free cash flow in the form of loans. Jack managed to save $2,000,000 of cash value in the process. Jack also put together a health savings account, which now has a value of $240,000 and can be used tax-free to pay additional medical expenses not covered by Medicare, or that can be taken as income and taxed as if it were an additional IRA.

---

[82] Lewis Schiff and Russ Alan Prince, "The Rise of the New Rich and How They Are Changing America," (February 2008) quoted by Belinda Goldsmith for Reuters, "More U.S. millionaires are middle-class," Reuters (October 31, 2007) [January 2, 2008].

Kate put away money in her IRA, which she grew with a good index program; it now has a value of $300,000. She and Jack have a home with a value of $850,000 and a remaining mortgage of $250,000 because they preferred to pay themselves before the bank and put money away knowing that the home would appreciate regardless. They also purchased two investment properties of which the combined value is now $1,200,000.

Both properties were purchased at $300,000 and over a twenty-year period, appreciated only fiver percent but were paid off by the renters. Keep in mind that Jack and Kate didn't harvest as much of the equity from the investment properties over the years as they could have and deployed into other compound building assets, so they missed out a little.

Can you see, through the example of Jack and Kate, the abundant retirement you can have if you've done proper planning? This is a conservative estimate and with an ordinary income, a couple was able to put away $4,540,000 in cash and assets and probably could have done a little more by taking full advantage of leverage, arbitrage and cash flow—the pillars that build wealth.

Use this example to examine your own circumstances. Jack and Kate built a diversified portfolio that took advantage of leverage (in their investment properties), cash (again, in the investment properties, and in their life insurance policy) and arbitrage (in their life insurance, IRA and other tax-advantaged assets). This is the kind of planning you should be looking at.

Many people spin their wheels during their working years, stuck in company retirement plans that cost too much to be of any real use, and fall victim to common mistakes made by managers. I personally think it is wise to do some additional planning.

You can get yourself started on earning supplemental income if you buy one investment property outside of your personal residence. You can also create deductions to offset your primary income if you work for someone else. If you don't think outside of the box and look inside the entrepreneur's box along with investing in the asset classes that make sense for your current worth, then you're probably not going to get to the retained lifestyle you're looking for.

I am not pooh-poohing all stock market assets. I want to make it clear that I think they have their place, and that when you have around $2,000,000 liquid, it could make sense to have proper management. I like the Fortuna Triangle model of management because it preserves cash flow and only in the very top, the smallest portion, do we bet against the market and take mammoth risks. Remember the theme of Benjamin Graham: look for something that protects the principal and provides an adequate return, and then you can move ahead full speed. Fail to do so and you can be dragged down to the bottom, like so many people were in 2000.

You CAN Prepare for Retirement on a Modest Income

My team and I have taken ordinary folks with only $300 to $400 to spend per month and designed future tax-free income streams for their retirements, twenty years away, of $15,000 a year or more for life. These are dollars that are not taxed each year of retirement. This tax-free income will be significant additions to their retirements, coupled with the IRA and real estate investments they can add to their portfolio. You can do the same.

What many of my clients will do with their investment properties is either refinance from time to time and adjust the rents so that they can take out tax-free cash in the form of loans, or do a 1031 exchange (tax-deferred exchange) that allows them to participate in large commercial buildings, which reduces stress since they never worry about the rents or any liabilities and are provided with fixed incomes for life that remain continuously deferred.

Most Are Not Prepared

As we head into the future, numbers are pointing to retiree income in 2030 being $45 billion short of need. However, saving an added five percent of income could protect you. This could mean that extra $300 or $400 per month for some of the people we've assisted.

A new study by the Employee Benefit Research Institute, titled "Can America Afford Tomorrow's Retirees?"[83] showed this to be the case, but projected a more dire situation for lower-income Americans, for whom saving twenty-five percent of their income might be necessary in order to be prepared for retirement.

According to the study, single women with low incomes are most at risk of falling short on retirement needs. People with higher incomes, or couples with dual incomes, will fare better, which seems like an obvious conclusion. But, there are ways for almost anyone to at least save a little bit, and I advise everyone to see financial planners to start preparing right now for when you retire.

What's the Answer?

What is the answer to lifestyle and retirement success? Simple. It starts with determination and a willingness to change and adopt new ideas. If you keep doing the same thing you've always been doing and you're not satisfied with the results, you need to change.

The use of investment-grade life insurance and real estate just makes sense, since you can use leverage; remember, leverage means "do more with less." If you don't think you need to do more with less than ever before, you're kidding yourself.

Investment-grade life insurance is not the same as the kind you get countless letters and spam e-mails about. This is life insurance that is focused on building up a triple compound for tax-free income, which is unlike anything your pension plan can do for you. The difference between the deferral that life insurance experiences and that of the pension plan is in the payout. Life insurance is received as a loan and considered tax-free. We are talking about real life insurance, not the typical death insurance that most people have, because this insurance *you* benefit from—not just your beneficiaries.

I do want to warn you: There are a number of insurance planners out there trying to do the planning in tandem with helping you manage your home equity, and they don't have a clue what they're

---

[83] Jack VanDerhei and Craig Copeland, Employee Benefit Research Institute, "Can America Afford Tomorrow's Retirees: Results From the EBRI-ERF Retirement Security Projection." EBRI Issue Brief #263, 2003.

doing. If you decide that taking a look at supplemental retirement income with indexed life insurance makes sense for you, remember to ask a few basic questions. The first question is, What percentage of the index does your product credit, and what is the cap? Also, can they explain to you the internal rate of return of the product, and are the insurance expenses descending or level? Then, ask them if they know how to optimize the policy beyond ordinary crediting. If they can't meet this litmus test, then run.

In the same way you want to run from poor insurance advisors, be leery of buying investment property off the Internet or through an e-mail blast. I've looked at numerous offerings like this and they almost never include the whole story. These people are looking for dummies who don't know enough to ask for all the numbers and don't have a clue how cash flow works. Remember what I said earlier: Promoters lie; the math doesn't, as long as you get good numbers. You need to question the numbers if they do not seem consistent.

Get into a membership with your local real estate investment club and don't buy anything on impulse. Go a few times and see if they feel legit to you, since some might only be in business to get a split off the deals they host.

> The teacher, if indeed wise, does not bid you to enter the house of their wisdom, but leads you to the threshold of your own mind.
> —Kahlil Gibran

What We Learned

1. Slow, methodical investing in vehicles that avoid the five destroyers of wealth and that compound over time often beat quick flashes in the pan (stock trades).

2. A comfortable retirement is going to be more difficult in the future—especially so for some classes.

3. Today's sixty-five-year-olds are a mix of fifty-four percent dependent, thirty-six percent working, five percent dead, four percent financially independent ($3,000 per month), and one percent wealthy.

4. Long-term care threatens to bankrupt Medicaid and the states that pay for it.

5. The five destroyers of wealth are: 1) Taxes, 2) Inflation, 3) Procrastination, 4) Expenses, and 5) Debt, and can be remembered through the mnemonic device TIPED.

6. The number of Americans worth $1 million to $10 million has risen to 8.4 million households or 7.6 percent of US households, and is growing at fifteen percent a year.

7. Retiree income in 2030 will be $45 billion short of need; but, saving an added five percent of income could protect many future retirees.

8. Putting together a retirement plan means looking at what opportunities are best for you—especially those that use the three pillars of wealth.

CHAPTER NINETEEN

How to Get the Ball Rolling

Getting started on a wealth building plan means knowing where you are and where you intend to arrive. Would a person driving across the country for the first time leave without mapping it? I hope your answer is "no". So, why would you go through life having no idea where you're headed financially? Let's face it: Without dough, retirement can be a pretty miserable place.

By now, you know that you have to look for opportunities to use the Three Secret Pillars of Wealth in your own situation, when you can. Along with that outlook, develop the habit of examining your finances in the form of a balance sheet and budget spreadsheet. I know you've heard that debt management is a key to getting ahead, and that's true. There is no magic to it, either, other than taking the same approach a company takes with its cash flow accountability. Who knows—you may find you have more capital than you thought for following the five steps.

So many businesses and individual investors who come to my office cannot answer my threshold question: "Where are you now financially, and where do you want to be five, ten or twenty years from now?" The reason they can't answer is because they have no vision, no plan. You may get away with being opportunistic in business for a while but ultimately, you have to become strategic, which means having a long-term vision. Investing and accumulating wealth is no different; you will not get where you want to be unless you know what the "where" is and what it looks like.

I don't really like to use the term "retirement" any longer because one day, I realized it was really lifestyle retention planning, rather than a plan for your last years. That change in outlook has simplified the planning process and now, the question is simple: What are you trying to accomplish, and where do you want to be in twenty years? Which is about the time you want to stop working.

When you stop working, I hope you want to retain your lifestyle to the extent your health allows, and no one I've ever talked to wanted to live like a little kid, waiting for their allowance from Uncle Sam (Social Security) or their former employer (pension check). You need to at least preserve your lifestyle so that the last years of your life are not filled with further struggle and dissatisfaction.

You have to be clear about what is important to you and your future, and how far you're prepared to go to commit to that vision and make it happen. Many people will read books like this and go, "That's great," or "He's nuts," but both groups will not act on any of it. I really want you to use this as a manual for thinking about and planning your financial future. My greatest ambition with this book is to have one or more people say, "Thanks—you inspired me to take a look at myself and now I'm on a path I never dreamed possible."

Ask yourself serious questions about what you want your retirement to look like and what you want to do with your time. The answers to those questions will dictate a lot of what you do now with your financial planning.

Please plan and keep in mind that setbacks and pitfalls will beset everyone, including you. I have people tell me all day long that real estate is the best investment and that they love real estate. I agree, and I always look for deals. However, at the time this book is being written, we're looking at a huge downturn in the real estate market without a clue as to how long it will last. We haven't seen the same economic factors before, so there is no credible information to go on.

Nevertheless, if wealth leaves any clues, and I believe it does, then real estate is a good place to look for wealth-building opportunities. Some of the most astounding wealth in the world has been created by real estate, and it may be on sale soon. But, even real estate has pitfalls, and you need to include contingencies in your financial plan.

Diversification is mentioned all the time in the financial industry, but the usual pie chart of allocation used by many financial planners has proven itself unproductive, otherwise many of the funds that usually comprise these allocations would have survived April 2000. What makes sense, and what my friend Karen Brenner of Fortuna Management and I agree on, is that you need variety in your plan to prevent depletion in your cash flows. If one market is down, you'd better have something else to compensate for the lost cash flow.

Markets often become completely unpredictable and having a safeguard is not only necessary, it is intelligent. I have to tell the real estate aficionado that I love real estate, too, but I'm going to be funding some dollars during a market downturn into a guaranteed product that preserves my principal and provides an adequate return despite what the market is doing. This idea of variety is not diversification in the same sense as a portfolio packed with mutual funds. This isn't diversification for diversification's sake. It's focused and limited to the investments that meet the criteria we've set out in the book up to this point.

Go ahead—get started and assess your finances right now. Stop and take a good, solid look at where you are and stop acting like an ostrich with its head buried in the sand. Learn how to calculate your cash flow as we discussed earlier, and remove as much bad debt from your finances as possible. Think like an investor and control your urge to splurge. By taking these tiny steps, you've started your journey to bigger and greater things. I hope to be the person who can applaud you and congratulate you for releasing the trapped investor inside yourself.

Ask yourself this series of questions to put yourself on track.

1. What is your discretionary income after expenses?

2. What is your vision for your future?

3. Do you want to retain your current lifestyle?

4. How much are you prepared to commit to get there?

5. Do you have any trapped dollars that are sitting in inefficient vehicles that once released, can be put to better use (e.g., home equity, an overfunded pension, or a business equity)?

6. Where can you get adequate education that will prepare you to deploy these funds?

7. Do you feel comfortable with real estate and products that use stock indexes to protect your principal and provide an adequate return?

8. Are you prepared to act on original ideas in order to survive and create an extraordinary outcome?

Did you find these questions difficult to answer? Were you able to answer all of them? Even if you had trouble answering these questions, you have at least begun the process of thinking seriously about your finances. If you don't learn anything else from this book, learn to live within your means, lower your monthly debt and run yourself like a mini-enterprise that has a balance sheet with cash flow. Accept nothing less than excellence from yourself.

You can live and have fun, but if you don't make a decision to commit to your future with a vision, you'll build exactly what that type of carelessness provides: a path to working in your sixties, seventies and eighties. If you're lucky and have a long enough life, you might find yourself still at work in your nineties.

The future of the global economy, especially America's, is no joke. We have the largest population of aging people that we've ever had, and they're going to be using all of the government' resources available to them. Many have not saved and are in bad health, and guess who gets to pay for all that?

The price of oil is nearly a $100 per barrel at the time of this writing and rising as fast as the other costs of living. Tax brackets are certain to go up as we bail out of trillions of dollars of debt. Living paycheck to paycheck and thinking that a pension plan, IRA or inheritance is going to bail you out is not a strategic plan. Alright, maybe a good inheritance works, but the rest of it is destined to keep you working for a very long time.

Get in a real estate investment club and with a financial planner who also recognizes real estate as an investment. If you feel that your local real estate club or financial planner just does not understand your needs, you have at least learned more than most just by reading the bullet points at the end of each chapter in this book. My office can assist you if you're in California, and you are welcome to contact us if you have any questions or are looking for a referral to a planner who can discuss your options, goals and vision.

Stay focused and make all your actions intentional as you follow your vision. If you need coaching, don't hesitate to stay in touch with my office. Even the most famous Olympic athletes and the most beautiful celebrities in the world need personal trainers to stay in shape, because they get tired or busy or life gets in the way. In order to have the type of success you deserve, you may need someone whom you can turn to or run investments by for another opinion. It's no sin to ask for help and receive it.

What We Learned

1. Companies and families should have a vision. A vision statement is the first step toward your goal of controlling the way you live after you stop working.

1. Until you clearly imagine and picture your future lifestyle, the "how" is meaningless.

1. You have to act unconventionally when the conventional wisdom is failing.

1. Find a financial planner who uses or can understand the planning quadrant so that nothing is left out. If you have $2 million or more, you'll want to find Fortuna Asset Management.

To be what we are, and to become what we are capable of becoming, is the only end of life.
—Robert Louis Stevenson

APPENDIX

BURNS FINANCIAL PLANNING QUADRANT

Real Estate • Residential • Commercial • Tenants in common	**Cash Flows** • Equity indexed universal life Annuities • Deeds of trust • Tax lien certificates • Corporate debt

Plans
• Defined Benefit
• Non-qualified
  Self-directed
  * IRA
  * 401k
• Professional Retirement Strategy™
	MMGT
	• Professional management: The client has at least $2,000,000 of liquid assets and requires more sophisticated techniques.
	• Premium finance of life insurance as a succession capital strategy to create liquidity in a large estate.

NCAIV*
* Asset-backed notes
* Energy
* Equipment leasing
* Real estate
* Managed futures

* NCAIV = Non-correlated Alternative Investment Vehicles.

The Burns Financial Quadrant is a system I came up with to make sure that all of your assets are acknowledged, and that nothing is left on the table when examining your wealth potential. Too often, financial institutions do not recognize your real estate because it is not a part of their commission grid. If these institutions were intelligent, they would incorporate an investment real estate component; I know one that is doing this right now and is going to be cutting-edge in the financial field.

Suggested Reading List and Resources

The Little Book of Common Sense Investing: The Only Way to Guarantee Your Fair Share of Stock Market Returns by John C. Bogle

Cashflow Quadrant: Rich Dad's Guide to Financial Freedom by Robert Kiyosaki

What's Your Net Worth?: Click Your Way to Wealth by Jennifer Openshaw

What Every Real Estate Investor Needs To Know About Cash Flow… And 36 Other Key Financial Measures by Frank Gallinelli

The 106 Common Mistakes Home Buyers Make (and How You Can Avoid Them) by Gary Eldred

How the Best Get Better by Dan Sullivan, the Strategic Coach.

The Retirement Savings Time Bomb…and How to Defuse It by Ed Slott

Small Business Cash Flow—Strategies for Making Your Business a Financial Success by Denise O'Berry

Decision Power—How to Make Successful Decisions with Confidence by Harvey Kaye

Timing the Real Estate Market by Robert Campbell

Sterling Trust Company (self-directed IRAs) http://www.sterling-trust.com/.